Enhancing Livelihood Security of Tribal Communities

About Authors

Dr. Shridhar Patil completed his graduation in Agriculture from University of Agricultural Sciences, Dharwad in the year 2008; MSc (Extension Education) from Mahatma Phule Krishi Vidhyapeeth in the year 2010, Rahuri and PhD (Agricultural Extension) from Indian Agricultural Research Institute, New Delhi in the year 2017. Since 2014 he is working as the Assistant Professor cum Junior Scientist at Bihar Agricultural University Sabour. He was awarded with Dr. G. Trivedi, Best Extension Professional Award by Bihar Agricultural Universtiy, Sabour for the year 2018-19.

Dr. Ravindra Kumar Sohane, is recipient prestigious awards ICAR- Swami Sahajanand Award, e-governance award by Govt. of India and many more. Currently he is Vice Chancellor of Bihar Agricultural University, Sabour, Bhagalpur, (Bihar). He was awarded Master's degree in the year 1990 and doctoral degree in the year 2000 with the specialization in the area of Animal Nutrition from GBPUA&T, Pantnagar. He is having vast experience in the area of farm extension, research and its management. He has served in the various positions including Scientist; District Project Coordinator of U.P. Diversified Agriculture Support Project; Training Organizer; Programme Coordinator etc. He has also worked as the Director, BAMETI, Patna. Since 2012, he is working as the Director Extension Education at the Bihar Agricultural University Sabour. He has to his credit more than 150 research and review papers, books book chapters, articles, bulletins publication in scientific journals.

Dr. Dharmendra Kumar did his graduation in Veterinary Sciences & Animal Husbandry in the year 2003 from Gujarat Agricultural University and Master's in animal nutrition from Bihar Veterinary College, Patna in the year 2006. He was awarded PhD degree in the year 2011. He has worked under Mother Dairy project at Junagarh for its Ration Balancing programme for dairy animals. Since 2012, he is working as Subject Matter Specialist (Animal Science) at Krishi Vigyan Kendra, Banka under Bihar Agricultural University, Sabour. He was awarded Best extension scientist award in 2020 by the Bihar Agricultuiral University, Sabour.

Dr. Hemant Kumar Singh has completed PhD in Horticulture (Olericulture) at the Bihar Agricultural University, Sabour, Bhagalpur. He has qualified the ICAR-ASRB NET and ICAR-SRF examinations. He was awarded with Best PhD Thesis Award (2017) and Best Extension Scientist Award (2019) by the Bihar Agricultural University, Sabour. He is currently working as the Subject Matter Specialist (Horticulture) in Krishi Vigyan Kendra, Kishanganj since 2015, under Bihar Agricultural University, Sabour (Bhagalpur), Bihar.

Enhancing Livelihood Security of Tribal Communities

Shridhar Patil
Assistant Professor cum Junior Scientist
Bihar Agricultural University
Sabour, Bhagalpur-813 210
Bihar

Ravindra Kumar Sohane
Vice Chancellor
Bihar Agricultural University
Sabour, Bhagalpur-813 210
Bihar

Dharmendra Kumar
Subject Matter Specialist (Animal Science)
Krishi Vigyan Kendra, Banka
Bihar Agricultural University
Sabour, Bhagalpur-813 210
Bihar

Hemant Kumar Singh
Subject Matter Specialist (Horticulture)
Krishi Vigyan Kendra, Kishanganj
Bihar Agricultural University
Sabour, Bhagalpur-813 210
Bihar

NEW INDIA PUBLISHING AGENCY
New Delhi-110 034

NEW INDIA PUBLISHING AGENCY
101, Vikas Surya Plaza, CU Block, LSC Market
Pitam Pura, New Delhi – 110 034, India
Email: info@nipabooks.com
Web: www.nipabooks.com

For customer assistance, please contact
Phone: + 91-11-27 34 17 17 Fax: + 91-11- 27 34 16 16
E-Mail: feedbacks@nipabooks.com

ISBN: 978-93-90512-00-3

Composed and Designed by NIPA.

Preface

The Ministry of Tribal Affairs was set up in 1999 with the purpose of carrying out the integrated socio-economic development of the Scheduled Tribes in a coordinated and planned manner across India. Bhuria Commission Report (2004) states that land and forests are the two basic resources of the tribal life- support system and there have been assaults on both. Agriculture and allied sectors are the integral part of the land based livelihood sources of tribal communities.

Bihar is the one of the states with lowest farm household income in the country and the state of affairs of tribal livelihood security is far poorer in the remotely located agriculture dependent rural tribal communities. The data on performance of tribal communities on the health and nutrition indicators shows that prevalence of child mortality, stunting, wasting of children and manifestations of nutritional deficiencies etc. are relatively high among the tribal communities. Further studies have shown that economic productivity of resources is also poor among these communities which is evident from lack of adoption of new technologies, low farm production and productivity, disguised unemployment, lack of diversity in farm activities and poor use of household resources. This situation calls for improving socioeconomic status of these communities through technological interventions, community mobilization and creation of community-based services and resources.

This book depicts planning, execution and outcome of one such project executed under Tribal Sub Plan Scheme by Bihar Agricultural University, Sabour with the purpose of creation and diversification of the income generating sources; capacity building of tribal men and women to undertake economically productive activities and creation in-house sustainable food systems that support the household food and nutritional security utilizing the locally available resources and homestead land and surrounding.

We are hopeful that the experiences and outcomes gained during execution of this project which are illustrated in this book will be helpful in planning, monitoring and evaluation of tribal development projects to the agencies working towards tribal development.

We are greatful to Dr. A.K. Singh Former Vice Chancellor, BAU, Sabour for his kind cooperation and inspiration in bringing out this publication. We are also thankful to the KVK Banka; KVK, Kishanganj and KVK, Kaithar for valuable contributions.

We are also thankful to Dr. P. S. Pandey, Assistant Director General (EP&HS) and Dr. Nidhi Verma, Principal Scientist, (EP&HS) Agricultural Education Division, ICAR New Delhi for their valuable assitance in implementation of the Tribal Sub Plan project.

Authors

Contents

1

Tribal Sub Plan: Origin and Concept[1]

Since the beginning of the Planning process, efforts have been made to ensure that the tribal people were included in the growth process. However, the strategy changed with each Five-Year Plan as new lessons were learnt from various developmental efforts. The First Five Year Plan emphasized the provision of additional financial resources through a community development approach to address the problems of tribal people rather than evolving a clear-cut tribal development strategy. Towards the end of the Plan (1954), 43 Special Multipurpose Tribal Development Projects (MTDPs) were created. These MTDPs could not fully serve the interest of the tribal people since the schemes were numerous and of a general nature. This approach continued during the second Five Year Plan. In the Third Plan, a different strategy for tribal development was evolved by converting the Community Development Blocks, where the concentration of tribal population was 66% and above, into Tribal Development Blocks (TDBs). By the end of the fourth Five Year Plan, the number of Tribal Development Blocks in the country rose to 504. The strategy of development through Tribal Development Blocks had its limitations as well, as it failed to address the cause of the tribal population of the country living outside the Tribal Development Blocks, which comprised more than 60% of the total tribal population. During the th on 5 Five Year Plan period, the exercise of identification of tribal majority blocks was undertaken. These were later constituted into 194 ITDAs/ITDPs in the country.

The present Tribal Sub Plan (TSP) strategy was initially developed by an Expert Committee set up by the Ministry of Education and Social Welfare in 1972 under the Chairmanship of Prof. S.C. Dube for the rapid socio-economic development of tribal people and was adopted for the first time in the Fifth Five Year Plan. The TSP strategy, with some modifications, continues till this day and the salient features concerning TSP for States, are given below:

[1]Contents of this chapter are adopted from the documents made available at its website by the National Commission for the Scheduled Tribes, Government of India.

i) The funds provided under the Tribal Sub Plan of the State have to be at least equal in proportion to the ST population of each State or UT

ii) Tribals and tribal areas of a State or UT are given benefits under the TSP, in addition to what percolates from the overall Plan of a State/UT

iii) The Sub-Plan should.

   a) Identify the problems and needs of tribal people and critical gaps in their development.

   b) Identity all available resources for TSP

   c) Prepare a broad policy framework for development,

   d) Prepare a detailed department wise plan

   e) Define a suitable administrative strategy for its implementation.

   f) Specify the mechanism for monitoring and evaluation.

iv) The TSP strategy has been in operation in 22 states and 2 UTs. However, funds meant for UTs are being provided for in the budget of the Ministry of Home Affairs since 2003-04 and therefore, the Ministry of Tribal Affairs is not concerned in the administration of TSP funds in the UTs.

v) TSP concept does not apply to the tribal majority States of Arunachal Pradesh, Meghalaya, Mizoram and Nagaland and in the UTs of Lakshadweep and Dadra & Nagar Haveli where tribals represent more than 60 % of the population, since the Annual Plan in these States/UTs is itself a Tribal Plan. A statement showing State-wise total and Scheduled Tribe population as per census 1991, 2001, and 2011 respectively is given at

Funding of Tribal Development Programmes under TSP

Funds for tribal development under TSP are sourced from: i) State Plans; ii) The Special area programmes of Special Central Assistance (SCA) to Tribal Sub Plan (TSP) and Grant under Article 275 (1) of the Constitution, as also the funds under the other Schemes of the Ministry; iii) Sectoral programmes of Central Ministries/ Departments; and iv) Institutional Finance.

TSP Components of States and UTs

The Planning Commission had issued guidelines for the States and UTs to earmark funds for TSP to be placed under a separate Budget Head Code 796 from total State/ UT Plan outlay. As per guidelines issued by the Planning Commission, the Tribal Sub Plan funds are to be non-divertible and non-lapsable. The guidelines also provide that the Tribal Welfare Department will be nodal Departments for the formulation and implementation of the Tribal Sub Plan in the States. Though the States are expected to provide under the TSP funds which are at least equal to the percentage of the tribal population to the total population in the State, and though the Ministry of Tribal Affairs and the Planning Commission have repeatedly laid stress on earmarking of adequate resources, some of the 3 States while preparing the Annual Plan for even 2013-14 have continued to allocate fewer than proportional resources to TSP.

TSP Components of Central Ministries/Departments

The TSP strategy is expected to be followed in the Central Ministries/ Departments also so that an adequate flow of funds in the Central Ministries/ Departments is ensured. Ministries/ Departments had earlier been reporting difficulty in implementing TSP citing indivisibility of projects, projects being applicable to all communities, including SCs/STs, etc. The Ministry of Tribal Affairs taking this into account had approached the Planning Commission for devising a different strategy for Central Ministries on TSP. The Planning Commission constituted a Task Force in June 2010 under the chairmanship of Dr. Narendra Jadhav, Member, Planning Commission. It recommended the classification of a specific list of Ministries/Departments according to their obligations regarding earmarking of Plan outlays for TSP.

Special Central Assistance (SCA) to the Tribal Sub- Plan

This is a major programme administered by the Ministry under which, grant is provided to the State Governments based on annual allocation made by the Planning Commission. This is treated as an additive to the State Plan, for areas where State Plan provisions are not normally forthcoming to bring about economic development to tribals. The programme was launched during 1974-75 and till the end of the IX Five Year Plan, the SCA to TSP was meant for filling up critical gaps in the family-based income-generating activities of TSP. From the Tenth Five Year Plan period, the objective and scope of SCA to TSP, was expanded to cover employment-cum-income generation activities and infrastructure incidental thereto. Beside family-based activities, other activities run by the Self-Help Groups (SHGs)/ Community are also to be taken up. The ultimate objective of extending SCA to TSP is to boost the demand-based income-generation programmes and thus raise the economic and social status of tribals. The guidelines for implementation by the States were revised in May 2003 and were further modified in January 2008. Recently in March 2014, the Ministry of Tribal Affairs has issued operational guidelines for the formulation, implementation, and monitoring of Tribal Sub-Plan and grants under Article 275(1) which has brought out certain substantive changes in the thrust of these Special Area Programmes, as also some procedural changes.

SCA is provided to 22 Tribal Sub-Plan States including the North Eastern States of Assam, Manipur, Sikkim and Tripura and two Union Territories. Since 2003-04 funds meant for UTs are being provided in the budget of the Ministry of Home Affairs and therefore, the Ministry of Tribal Affairs is not concerned with the administration of funds in the UTs. Funds under 4 SCA to TSP are released for economic development in the following areas and for the following population: -

(i) ITDP/ITDA areas (194 Nos.), which are generally contiguous areas of the size of at least tehsil or block or more in which the ST population is 50% or more of the total population

(ii) MADA pockets (259 Nos.), which are identified pockets having 50% or more ST population with a minimum population of 10,000

(iii) Clusters (82 Nos.), which are identified pockets having 50% ST population with a minimum population of 5,000

(iv) Particularly Vulnerable Tribal Groups (PTGs), characterized by a low rate of growth of population, pre-agricultural level of technology, and an extremely low level of literacy

(v) Dispersed tribal population - those tribals who fall outside the categories at Sl No.(i) to (iv) above

The Ministry provides 100% grant-in-aid to State Governments from the SCA funds made available to the Ministry for the purpose annually by the Planning Commission. Funds to the level of Rs. 15.00 Lakhs per village under the program for Development of Forest Villages were also provided as an extension of the Special Central Assistance to Tribal SubPlan (SCA to TSP). The government has decided that additional funding up to Rs. 15.00 Lakh each would be provided to all those forest villages which have availed the first phase funding during the Xth Plan.

Grants under the First Proviso to article 275(1) of the Constitution

The Ministry of Tribal Affairs provides grants to 22 Tribal Sub-Plan and 4 tribal majority States under the First Proviso to article 275(1) of the Constitution to meet the cost of such projects for tribal development as may be undertaken by the State Governments for the promoting the welfare of the Scheduled Tribes in the State and for raising the level of administration of the Scheduled Areas therein to that of the rest of the State. Since 1997-98, it has been decided to utilize a part of the funds under Article 275(1) of the Constitution for setting up 100 Model Residential Schools (named as Eklavya Vidyalaya) from class 6th to 10th in States & UTs for tribal students. For this purpose, Rs.150.00 crores were earmarked during the 9th Five Year Plan out of the funds available under

Article 275(1) of the Constitution. The objective of setting up of the Eklavya Vidyalayas is to provide quality education to the tribal students. 164 Eklavya Vidyalayas were sanctioned to 22 States up to 31/03/2014 since the beginning and 120 Schools are reported to be functional

A fixed grant under the second proviso to Article 275(1) of the Constitution (NonPlan) is given to the Government of Assam in respect of the administration of tribal areas in the hill districts of North Cachar and Karbi Anglong.

2

Status of Scheduled Tribes in Bihar

Bihar state is located in the Eastern part of the country and has a total geographical area of 94,763 Sq km which accounts for 2.85% of the country's total land area. Out of the total geographical area, 57.12 lakh hectares is under cultivation, which accounts for 60.27% of the total geographical area. The Gross and net sown area in the state is 78.82 and 57.12 lakh ha, respectively and presently the cropping intensity is about 138%. Paddy, wheat, pulses, maize, potato and oilseeds are the major field crops of the state, while mango, litchi and banana are the major fruit crops. As the third-largest vegetable producer, the state accounts for eight percent of Indian vegetable basket. Among the livestock sector, cow and buffalo are the majorly dairy animals. Goatery and poultry are also practiced on a wide scale in the state. Agriculture and its allied sectors together account for about one third (33.00%) of the State's Gross Domestic Product (GDP). This makes agriculture an important source of livelihood and a potential instrument for the attainment of inclusive, grassroots level and widespread developmental change.

Bihar State is characterized by its high population density, largely dependent on agriculture for livelihood. Its bountiful natural resources of fertile soil, abundant water and varied climatic conditions make Bihar an agriculturally high potential region. But, factors like fragmented and small landholdings, poor crop management practices, weaker market connectivity, lack of alternative sources of income, poor professional skills, absence of farm-level processing & value addition and poor investment possibilities in agriculture and allied sectors are resulting in widespread poverty among the rural masses of the state, which is more obvious among the scheduled tribe and scheduled caste population. There are around 1.47 crore landholdings in the State of which around 91.06 percent are marginal holdings of size less than 1 hectare (Agriculture Census, 2011). In addition to the above mentioned factors, lack of accessibility to productive resources and quality inputs, shortage of vocational skill development opportunities are the major contributory factors to the wide spread poverty in the state.

Demographic status of Scheduled Tribe in Bihar

As per Census, 2011 total population of Bihar state is 104.10 million of which 1.34 million people belong to scheduled tribes, constituting 1.28 % of the state population. More than 95% of the Scheduled tribe population is residing in rural parts of the state.

Out of twenty-nine (29) listed scheduled tribes of the state, Santhal is the most populous tribe, having a number of 367,612, constituting 48.5 percent of the total ST population of the State. Oraon and Kharwar are the second and third largest tribes, having a population of 1.20 and 1.07 Lakh, respectively. Along with Santhal, Oraon and Khanwar, Gond and Munda constitute 86.8 percent of the total tribal population. The figures in the above table indicate that the Scheduled Tribe population is concentrated mainly in few districts like Katihar, Purnea, Banka, Jamui, Bhagalpur, West Champaran, Kaimur and Rohtas. Katihar district has the highest proportion of STs (5.9 percent) followed by Jamui (4.8 percent), Banka (4.7 percent) and Purnia (4.4 percent).

Socio-economic and occupational status: Literacy among the Scheduled Tribes of Bihar is dismally low. The overall literacy rate of STs is 28.20 %, which is far below the state average of more than 65%. Surveys have revealed that the majority of the Scheduled Tribe population is engaged in low income-generating and non-skill labour activities. As per Census, 2001 Majority (62.50%) of the Scheduled Tribe population in Bihar state is engaged in agriculture as agriculture-workers. According to the latest poverty estimates for 2011-12 prepared by the Planning Commission, Scheduled Tribes (47.4 percent) suffer the highest level of poverty among social groups in rural areas. According to the Agricultural Census of 2005-06, the concentration of marginal holdings in Bihar is very high in the case of Scheduled Castes (95%) and Scheduled Tribes (88%). Far worse fact is that more than two lakh SC/ST families don't even have homestead land. The representation of Scheduled Tribes in institutions of local self-governance of Bihar is to just to the tune of 0.77%. Food and nutritional security among the tribal communities in the Bihar is miserable with a Maternal Mortality rate of 30, Infant Mortality rate of 82.

As discussed above, the tribal population in Bihar state is characterized by lower literacy rates, lack of political and social bargaining power, lack of access to productive resources and vocational knowledge-skill development opportunities. These disadvantageous situations coupled with lack of adequate awareness, knowledge, skill and technological support system and the dependence on single source of livelihood have resulted in widespread low productivity, lower income and poor living condition among scheduled tribes of the state.

Government schemes, financial assistance or reservation provisions alone cannot be instrumental in improving educational status, access to the productive resources and enhancement of the income of tribal communities on a sustainable and inclusive basis. In order to bring about statewide systematic and sustainable improvement in the socio-economic condition of the tribal communities, the precondition is the adequacy and stability of the livelihood source.

Scheduled Tribe (ST) constitutes a considerable portion of Bihar state's population. There are more than 1.33 million Schedule Tribe residents in Bihar, constituting 1.28% of the state's total population. More than 95% of the tribal population of Bihar state lives in rural areas and the source of livelihood for the majority of these people are agriculture and related occupations. They are dependent on agriculture in the form of cultivators, agricultural labourers and producers of minor agro-products. Their source of livelihood is characterized by resource-poor small holdings, poorly developed livelihood infrastructure, lack of investment, uncertainties in production-marketing and low returns. These situational parameters make their livelihood source —the agriculture and its allied sectors — an uncertain and insufficient means of earning a livelihood. This calls for urgent intervention for increasing the robustness of livelihood sources and attainment of sustainability in income through improvisation of existing livelihood sources and diversification of income through the promotion of additional income-generating activities keeping '*agriculture and allied sectors*' at the central stage.

3

Conceptualization of Project under Tribal Sub Plan

For achieving the inclusive and sustainable development of the tribal communities in the selected areas we believe that imparting technical know-how of improved agricultural practices, development of vocational skills among rural resource-poor schedule tribes and ensuring the availability of quality technological input material will be instrumental. Considering these facts, in order to enhance the livelihood of the tribal communities in the selected district of Bihar this intervention project was designed with the following objectives.

Objectives

- Increasing agricultural production and productivity through the dissemination of appropriate resource and location-specific agricultural technologies.
- Enhancement of livelihood and nutritional security of tribal communities through agro-enterprise diversification.
- Enhancement of farm profitability among tribal communities through the promotion of value addition, agripreneurship and market linkage
- Professional and entrepreneurial empowerment of tribal communities through mobilization and organization of tribal men, women and youth into primary producer groups

To achieve these objectives gambit of interventions were included considering the socio-economic status of the potential beneficiaries. This included interventions like dissemination of improved farm production technologies including but not limited to high yielding and low input requiring improved varieties, efficient and cost-effective plant protection and post-harvest management practices; establishment of Backyard Kitchen Gardens for enhancement of nutritional security; diversification of agro enterprise through introduction of Beekeeping, Mushroom cultivation, Backyard poultry & livestock rearing and capacity building and skill development oriented vocational training programmes.

The primary criteria for the selection of beneficiaries was that the household should be of Scheduled Tribe as per the provision of Govt. of India. For each of the households in the list of Scheduled Tribe population, the interventions will be later on designed considering the interest, resources and socioeconomic situations of the household.

Nature of household and target intervention

Sl. No.	Nature of Household	Intervention
1.	Schedule tribe farmers with small/ marginal landholding	Cultivation of off-season vegetables By adoption of improved management practices
2.	Landless agricultural labourers with less time to invest in additional income generating activities	Mushroom cultivation Beekeeping
3.	Unemployed youth with entrepreneurial interests	Vocational skill development for milk production, processing and value addition
4.	Underemployed agricultural youth	Goatery, Beekeeping,
5.	Resource-poor women of landless families	Backyard poultry, Kitchen gardening
6.	Tribal farmer groups	Water harvesting ponds, micro-irrigation, polyhouse and protected cultivation, the introduction of new crops/cropping systems

Objective-wise activities, outputs and expected outcomes of the project

Objectives	Activities	Output	Outcome
Increasing agricultural production and productivity through the dissemination of appropriate resource and location-specific agricultural technologies and	Agroecosystem analysis and development of farm plan	Development of understanding about farming situation and identification of production constraints	Enhancement in agricultural production
	Promotion of pulse crops and short duration rice/wheat verities	Intensification of cropping systems	
	Dissemination of appropriately integrated nutrient and pest management practices	Reduction in yield loss due to nutrient mismanagement and insect pest attack	
	Development of village-level farm implement bank	Farm mechanization	

Objectives	Activities	Output	Outcome
Enhancement of livelihood and nutritional security of tribal communities through agro-enterprise diversification	Creating awareness among farmers and motivating them to adopt low investment agro enterprises	Diversification of livelihood sources	Enhancement of livelihood and nutritional security
	Training of tribal men and women for management of kitchen garden, mushroom cultivation, beekeeping, backyard poultry, goatery and dairy enterprise		
	Facilitation of market management	Income stability	
Enhancement of farm profitability among tribal communities through promotion of value addition, agripreneurship and market linkage	Awareness programmes	Increased awareness about the importance and role of value addition in income enhancement	Enhancement of farm profitability as a result of the establishment of food processing and value addition units
	Vocational training programmes on value addition	Development of skills and knowledge among farmers for food processing and value addition	
	Facilitation of linkage between farmers and financial agencies	Provision of capital for the establishment of value addition and food processing units	
Professional and entrepreneurial empowerment of tribal communities through mobilization and organization of tribal men, women and youth.	Mobilization of tribal communities into coherent groups	Organizational power to the tribal communities	Development of tribal communities into professional entrepreneurs
	Providing group management training to the farmers	Stabilization of groups	
	Providing group orientated extension services, vocational skills and consultancy services	Transformation of social groups into economic interest groups	

About Geographical Area

Banka district is located in agro-climatic zone IIIA and characterised by fine loamy soils with annual rainfall of 1170mm. The districts of Katihar and Kishanganj are characterised by Coarse loamy and Fine sandy soils with relatively higher average rainfall (1298mm and 2141mm, respectively). In Banka, of the total area, only 39 percent area is under crop cultivation which is far lower as compared state's average area under crop cultivation (55.60 %). The proportion of cultivable wasteland is also relatively high in Banka district. The area under forest cover is very little (< 1 percent) in both Kishanganj and Katihar districts as compared to state's average. Further analysis of land use planning also revealed that, cropping intensity was relatively low in Banka (125 %), Kishanganj (140 %), as well as Katihar (140 %) as compared to the states, average cropping intensity (146 %). Besides poor cropping intensity, the selected district's land-use patterns were also characterized by little area under tree fruits crops; a high proportion of barren & uncultivable lands (6-14%) and a high proportion of cultivable wastelands.

This situation of a smaller proportion of area under cultivation; large cultivable wastelands; low cropping intensity; little area under forest & tree fruit crops; a high proportion of barren & uncultivable lands and high proportion of cultivable wastelands indicate poor land resource use efficiency and call for interventions aimed at enhancing cropping intensity and increasing area under tree fruit crop and forest cover.

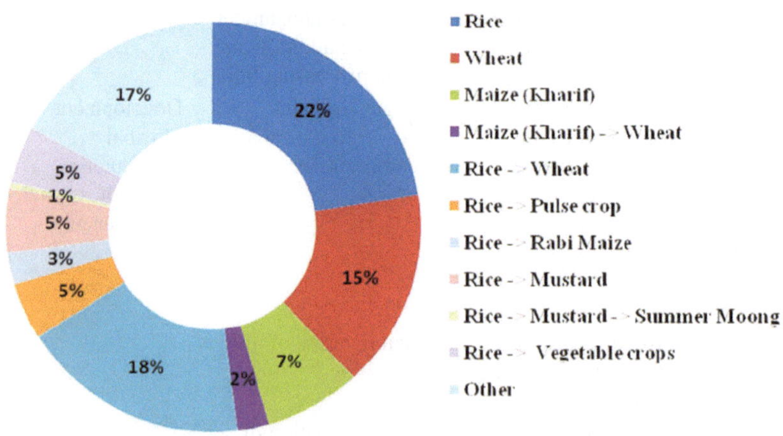

Land use pattern of Banka district

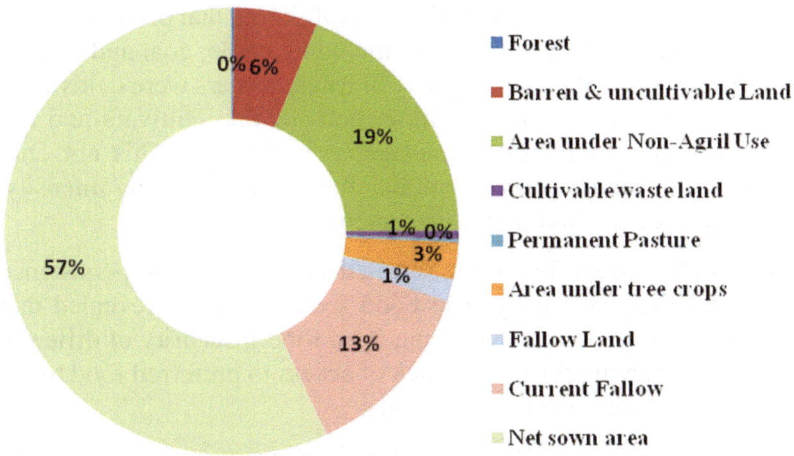

Land use pattern of Kishanganj district

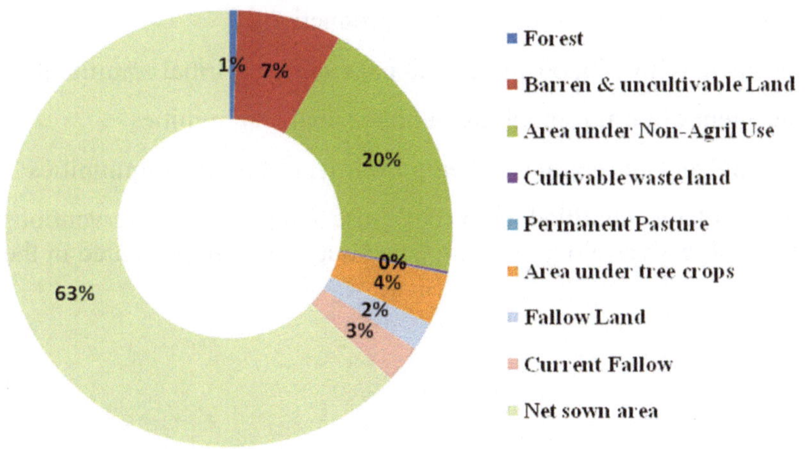

Land use pattern of Katihar district

In, addition to the inherent challenges and constraints of the study area, the baseline survey also revealed the significant problems and researchable issues that contribute to the low income, poor natural resource productivity and poor quality of life.

The baseline survey of selected villages revealed that tribal households have relatively low income (Rs. 3699/month) which is far lower than the average farm household income at the state as well as the national level. Further, it was also observed that the contribution of additional income generating allied activities to total income is too low which also has increased the financial instability and poor buffer capacity.

Coming to farm production & productivity, it was observed that productivity of major field crops as well as that of livestock including cattle, goat and poultry was very low. In addition to this, the majority of tribal farmers were cultivating single crop in a year, adopting low yielding non-suitable cultivars and not adopted scientific crop and livestock management practices. This not only resulted in poor use of land resources but also in reduced cropping intensity, lowering of total production and poor livestock productivity.

Another major problem identified in the selected villages was the persistence of malnutrition and food insecurity. The Food security survey revealed that more than half of households were suffering from food insecurity of different forms starting from worrying for food to lack of access to preferred food to the consumption of either small meals or no meals.

Based on problems identified following objectives were conceived for the project

1. Increasing agricultural production and productivity
2. Enhancement of livelihood and nutritional security of tribal communities
3. Enhancement of farm profitability among tribal communities
4. Professional and entrepreneurial empowerment of tribal communities

The details of problems identified, their root cause and proposed interventions to achieve these objectives along with expected outcomes are presented in the table below.

Conceptual Framework of the Project

Problem identified & their root cause	Activities & input	Output	Outcome & impact	Verifiable impact indicators
Poor land-use efficiency 1. Low cropping intensity 2. large cultivable wastelands 3. Underutilization of barren lands	1. Introduction of short duration rice & enabling early sowing of wheat 2. Demonstration of summer moong cultivation 3. Planting of fruit trees crops in barren lands 4. Use of homestead land for vegetable cultivation	1. Increase inc cropping intensity 2. Reduction in the area under barren and wastelands	Increase in land-use efficiency	1. Change in cropping intensity (%) 2. Additional area bough under cultivation (ha)
Low household income 1. Overdependence on wage labour 2. Poor income source diversification 3. Absence of allied farm activities	1. Vocational skill development among rural youth 2. Promotion of additional income-generating activities like beekeeping, mushroom cultivation and backyard poultry	1. Increase in the number of income sources and reduction of dependence on agriculture and wage labour for income earning	Enhanced farm income	Change in income (Rs/annum)
Poor productivity of field crops 1. Adoption of long duration varieties 2. Delayed & erratic monsoon 3. Terminal heat stress 4. The poor seed replacement rate 5. Lack of adoption of scientific crop management practices 6. The inability of farmers to make the best use of land resources in extreme weather conditions including submerged conditions	1. Promotion of early maturing Sahabhagi Dhan 2. Demonstrating the effect of early sowing of wheat 3. Ensuring the supply of quality seeds of HYVs 4. Organizing of Kisan chaupals for scientific farm knowledge dissemination 5. Introduction of Abiotic stress-tolerant crop varieties	1. Reduction in crop duration 2. Timely sowing of crops 3. Adoption of stress-tolerant varieties	Enhancement in crop productivity	Change in crop yield (q/ha)

Problem identified & their root cause	Activities & input	Output	Outcome & impact	Verifiable impact indicators
Poor livestock productivity 1. Nonadoption of scientific feed management practices 2. Lack of availability of green fodder round the year 3. Nonadoption of vaccination and lack of access to veterinary services 4. Lack of awareness about livestock disease prevention & control measures 5. Non-adoption of concentrated feed, mineral mixture and value-added animal feed and fodder materials including animal chocolates, silage and hay making	1. Paravet training programmes 2. Establishment of community livestock health centers 3. Livestock owner-scientist interaction meets 4. Vaccination and animal health camps 5. Demonstration of feed block, mineral mixtures and concentrated feed technologies 6. Demonstration of fodder crop cultivation in submerged lands	1. Creation of local veterinary service providers 2. Increase in awareness about animal nutrition and health management practices 3. Adoption of scientific livestock management practices 4. Reduction in livestock mortality rates	1. Increase in access to livestock health services 2. Improved animal health 3. Increase in livestock productivity	1. Increase in Milk yield (lit/animal/ICP) 2. Meat production (kg/animal), 3. Eggs laid (No./Yr) 4. No. of entrepreneurial opportunities created for trained paravet service providers 5. No. of community livestock health centres established
Poor rate of technology adoption 1. Lack of awareness about scientific practices 2. Lack of skill required for the adoption of scientific practices 3. Lack of technological credibility 4. Lack of access to quality input 5. Poor extension contact and lack of cosmopoliteness	1. Organization of exposure visits, interface meetings, technology demonstrations and handholding support 2. Creating provision for quality input material including seeds, fertilizers, mushroom spawns, planting material etc.	1. Strengthening of extension contact 2. Increase in awareness of scientific crop and livestock management practices 3. Access quality farm input 4. Increase in trust over technology	Increase in extent of adoption of farm and livestock management technologies	Change in extent of adoption of livestock and crop management practices

Problem identified & their root cause	Activities & input	Output	Outcome & impact	Verifiable impact indicators
Household food insecurity 1. Lack of in house fruit, vegetable and meat production systems 2. Absence of backyard poultry 3. Lack of awareness about scientific nutrition management practices	Promotion of backyard poultry, mushroom cultivation, kitchen gardening	Increase in availability of fruits, vegetables, meat and egg for household consumption	Increase in consumption of fruits, vegetables, meat and egg for household consumption	HFISA index

Salient features of the approach for tribal farming system improvement.

Capacity building and skill development through regular organization of training programs, awareness camps, field exposure and hands on experience of campus training

Enhancing extension contact, cosmopoliteness and technological exposure of tribal households through regular organization of scientist-farmer interaction meets, exposure visit, educational tour to KVKs, farmers' fields, seminars and Kisan Mela.

Income source diversification and enhancing of household food security through Promotion of Kitchen gardening; Backyard Poultry, Beekeeping and Mushroom cultivation

Enhancement of land utility through hydroponic fodder cultivation; planting of tree fruit crops in waste lands and homestead area and promotion of green fodder cultivation in submerged cultivable waste lands

Creating access to veterinary services and enhancing livestock productivity through capacity building of rural youth for developing rural paravet service providers; Establishment of community livestock health centres; Replacement of non-discrete poultry birds with Vanraja & Grampriya; Organization of awareness camps and livestock vaccination drives and demonstration of animal nutrition management technologies including feed block, animal chocolate, silage & hay making and use of mineral mixture

Enhancement of cropping intensity through promotion of summer moong cultivation; and replacement of Paddy-Maize cropping system with Paddy-Mustard-Moong

Enhancement of field crop productivity through Promotion of short duration and Abiotic stress tolerant (draught & submergence) paddy varieties; Enhancing of seed replacement ratio by ensuring timely supply of quality seed material and Demonstration of scientific crop management practices

Tribal villages / tribal farmers targeted

District	CD Block	Village
Banka	Banka	Dudhiyatari
		Manjhladih
		Khirkitari
	Katoriya	Nakti
		Budwabathan
		Longay
		Menkadih
		Jamua
	Bounsi	Kaniket
		Kalhajor
		Barapaghar
		Kiskiliya
		Mastmara
	Fullydumar	Bhalguha
		Narhatari
		Banarchuwa
		Kaithadol
		Gobardaha
		Birnadih
	Chandan	Babumahal
		Paharpur
		Dhawana
		Dumardiha
Kishanganj	Thakurganj	Baserbati
		Kudarbaghi
		Pathariya
		Hulhuli
		Sakhuadali
	Pothiya	Panasi
		Pokhariya
		Mahsul
		Sarogora
Katihar	Manihari	Nima

4

Research/Extension Work Organization Under Tribal Sub Plan

The extension/research work organization consisted of seven distinct steps namely,

1. Situation analysis
2. Identification of problems and setting up of objectives
3. Designing of interventions
4. Preparing plan of work & implementation of project interventions
5. Monitoring of implementation process
6. Impact assessment
7. Project reconsideration

Situation analysis: The project work was initiated with the collection of secondary information related to demography as well as the socio-economic condition of the project districts followed by a series of farmer scientist interaction meetings in the selected village clusters. These discussions were followed by a participatory rural appraisal and baseline survey. In order to prepare a statement of the situation, the focused group discussion method was utilized. Based on situation analysis the problems were identified and objectives set as described under.

Preliminary visits made to identify the villages

Participatory rural appraisal in the tribal village of Banka district

Identification of problems and setting up of objectives: Based on participatory rural appraisal as well as baseline surveys the problem identification process was begun. Once the observable problems and constraints were identified, the problem analysis was carried out and problem trees were developed. On the basis of detailed efforts following set of problems were identified.

Poor land-use efficiency due to low cropping intensity, large cultivable wastelands, and underutilization of lands

Low household income due to overdependence on wage labour, poor income source diversification and absence of allied farm activities

Poor productivity of field crops due to adoption of long duration varieties, delayed and erratic monsoon, terminal heat stress, poor seed replacement rate, lack of adoption of scientific crop management practices and the inability of farmers to make the best use of land resources in extreme weather conditions including submerged conditions

Poor livestock productivity due to non-adoption of scientific feed management practices, lack of availability of green fodder round the year, non-adoption of vaccination and lack of access to veterinary services, lack of awareness about livestock disease prevention & control measures and non-adoption of concentrated feed, mineral mixture and value-added animal feed and fodder materials including animal chocolates, silage and hey making.

Poor rate of technology adoption due to lack of awareness about scientific practices, lack of skill required for adoption of scientific practices, lack of technological credibility, lack of access to quality input and poor extension contact and lack of cosmopoliteness.

Household food insecurity due to lack of in house fruit, vegetable and meat production systems, absence of backyard poultry and lack of awareness about scientific nutrition management practices.

Setting up of objectives

Based on series of discussions with stakeholders following specific, measurable, attainable, relevant and time-bound (SMART) objectives were set for the project.

1. Increasing agricultural production and productivity
2. Enhancement of livelihood and nutritional security of tribal communities
3. Enhancement of farm profitability among tribal communities
4. Professional and entrepreneurial empowerment of tribal communities

Designing of interventions

The problems in the identified villages were discussed with subject matter specialists and appropriate interventions and intervention packages were designed to suit the socio-economic condition, cultural values as well as the resources available with tribal households. The brief account of interventions designed is given below.

1. Promotion of pulse crops and short duration rice/wheat verities
2. Creating awareness among farmers and motivating them to adopt low investment agro enterprises
3. Training of tribal men and women for management of kitchen garden, mushroom cultivation, beekeeping, backyard poultry, goatery and dairy enterprise
4. Creating provision for providing paravet services at the village level
5. Dissemination of scientific livestock nutrition and health management practices
6. Increasing resource use efficiency through crop intensification and bringing additional area under cultivation

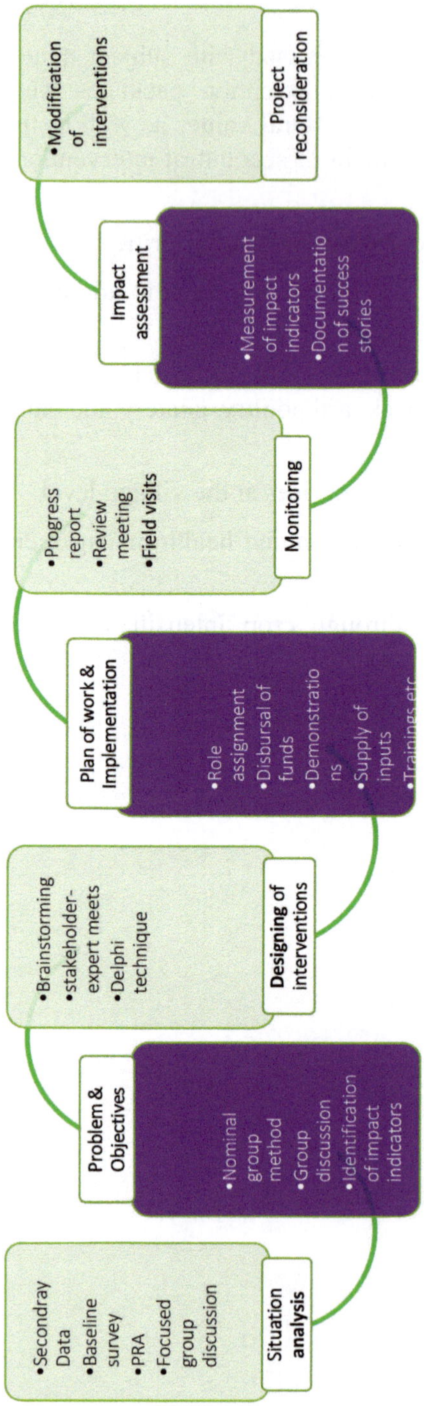
Situation analysis
•Secondray Data
•Baseline survey
•PRA
•Focused group discussion
Problem & Objectives
•Nominal group method
•Group discussion
•Identification of impact indicators
Designing of interventions
•Brainstorming
•stakeholder-expert meets
•Delphi technique
Plan of work & Implementation
•Role assignment
•Disbursal of funds
•Demonstrations
•Supply of inputs
•Trainings etc
Monitoring
•Progress report
•Review meeting
•Field visits
Impact assessment
•Measurement of impact indicators
•Documentation of success stories
Project reconsideration
•Modification of interventions

5

Socio-Economic Impact Assessment

Socio-economic impact assessment is an important activity that justifies the implementation and continuation of the project efforts and to enhance the observed ability of the project outcomes. there are several approaches available for assessment of the impact of project interventions. in the present investigation, before or after research design was used for impact assessment.

Socio-economic impact assessment activity, the benchmark survey boss carried out before the initiation of the project. The benchmark survey focused on the socio-economic profile of tribal households in the project area including the landholding, personal profile of the household head, household income, its sources, income source diversity. The survey also focused on the agronomical aspects like the productivity of major crops, cropping intensity and income generation from various farm activities. Further, in the benchmark survey, data was also collected on the aspects related to household food security. The findings of the benchmark survey are presented below.

Landholding

The baseline survey revealed that among sampled households large majority of respondents had less than a hectare land. One-third of the respondents had less than half a hectare of land, while only 13.33 percent of the sampled households had landholdings larger than 2 ha. Further, it was also observed that landholdings were not just small but also fragmented.

Size of landholding	% of households
Less than 0.5 ha	32.22
0.5 to < 1.0 ha	36.11
1.0 to 2.0 ha	18.33
> 2.0 ha	13.33

Age of household head

Age of household head (yrs)	% of households
Less than 25 yrs	11.11
25 to less than 46 yrs	38.89
46 to less than 66 yrs	37.78
66 years or more	12.22

Type of family

Type of family	% of households
Nuclear	68.33
Joint	31.67

Family size

Size of family	% households
04 or less	18.89
05 to 07	43.33
08 to 11	25.00
More than 11	12.78

Household income

Analysis of income source diversity in the project area prior to initiation of the project revealed that **unskilled wage labour earnings are the largest contributors to household income** (37 %), while crop cultivation contributes merely one third (35%) to the total income. The contribution of livestock and poultry to the income was found to be moderately well (19%). However, it was observed that the **contribution of allied farm activities to household income was very low (4%)** which contributed only Rs. 1776 per annum. **The average monthly income of the household was as low as Rs. 3699 only**.

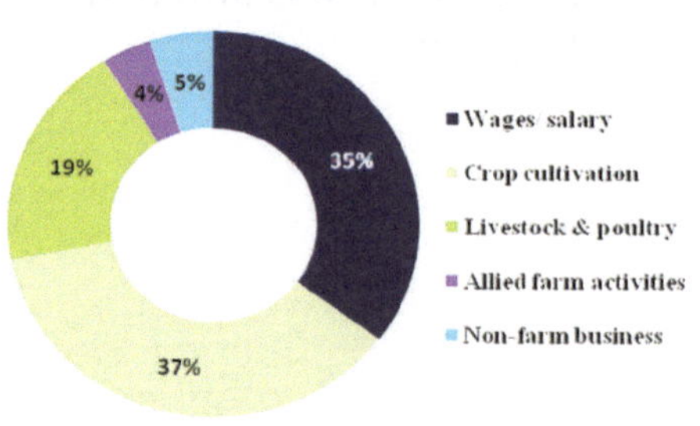

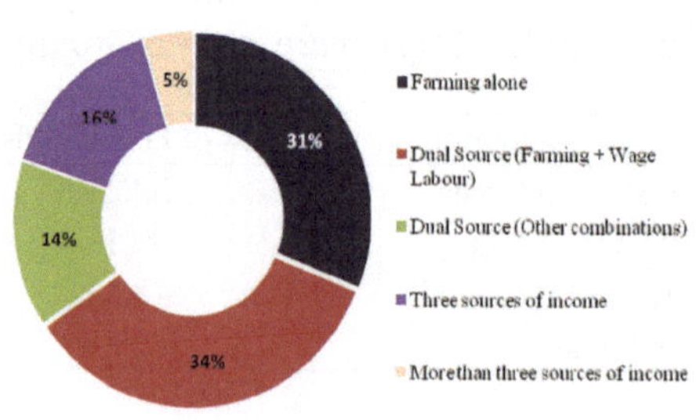

Utilization of land resources

A baseline survey of the selected villages revealed that more than 62 percent of the cultivated area is sown only once, while only 37 percent of the area is sown twice. Notably, less than one percent of the total cultivated area was sown all over the three seasons of *Kharif, Rabi* and *Zaid.* Rice, wheat and maize constitute major crops of the region. Of the 62 percent area where only one crop is cultivated in a year, the 22 percent area was under rice, 15 percent area was under Wheat, 7 percent area was under Maize crop cultivation. Of 37 percent area where double cropping was practiced, 18 percent area was under the Rice-Wheat cropping system followed by 5 percent area under Rice-Pulse crop.

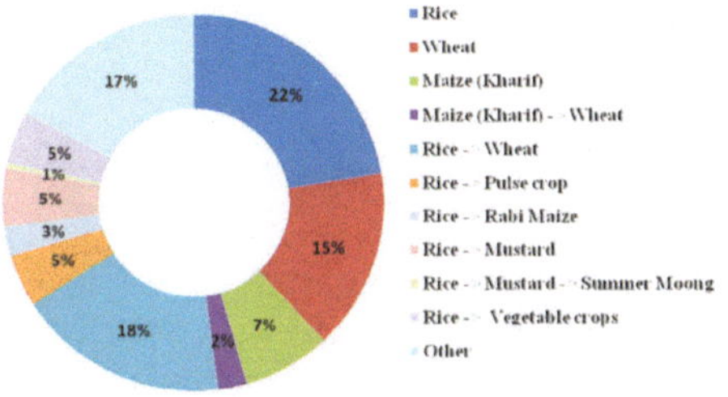

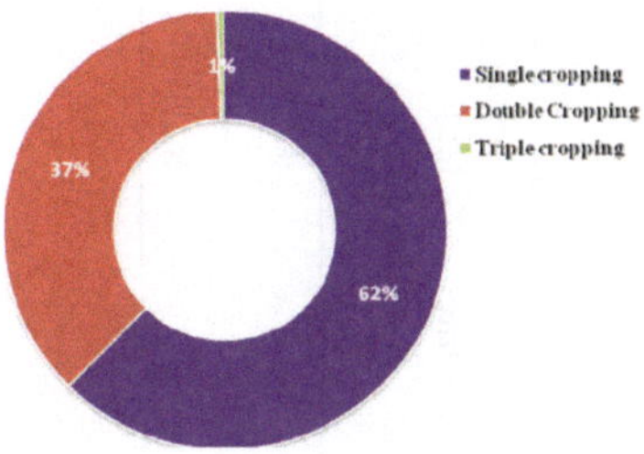

Field crops grown and their productivity

Crop	Paddy	Wheat	Maize (Kharif)	Maize (Rabi)	Gram	Mustard
Productivity	20.00 qt/ha	16.42 qt/ha	36.25 qt/ha	39.52 qt/ha	9.52 qt/ha	5.6 qt/ha

The low household income was due to poor crop productivity, poor livestock productivity and lack of income source diversification. During the baseline survey it was observed that the average productivity of Paddy, Wheat, Kharif Maize, Rabi Maize, Gram and Mustard were 20 quintal, 16.42 quintal, 36.25 quintal, 39.5 quintal, 9.5 quintal and 5.6 quintal per hectare, respectively. The low farm productivity was due to

1. Delayed onset of monsoon and erratic monsoon, especially in Banka district
2. Adoption of long duration varieties which are unable to tolerate water stress
3. Terminal heat stress due to delayed sowing of wheat
4. Poor seed replacement rate across all the crops and
5. Lack of adoption of scientific crop management practices including a selection of varieties.
6. The inability of farmers to make the best use of land resources in extreme weather conditions including submerged conditions

The baseline survey also revealed that alongside crops, the productivity of livestock was also poor. It was observed that almost the entire livestock population including cattle, goat, poultry and pig was constituted by non-discrete breeds. Most of the farmers were not following scientific livestock feed and health management practices. As a result of which it was observed

Livestock productivity

Livestock/ poultry	Cow/Buffalo	Goat				Poultry	
Parameter	Cattle Milk productivity (lit/inter- calving period)	Goat Meat (@ marketing age)	Goat Prolificacy rate	Goat Parturition rate	Goat Kid mortality rate	No. of eggs laid/yr	Bodyweight (gm)
Performance measure	398	6.05	1.5	1.6	30%	42.52	880
	878	7.68	1.75	2.0	13 %	82.59	2260

that, average milk productivity was only 398 liter/inter-calving period, the weight of goat meat at marketing age was 6 kg only, prolificacy rate and parturition rate among goat were 1.50 and 1.60, respectively. The goat kid mortality rate was as high as 30 percent. In the case of poultry, it was observed that the average number of eggs laid by bird annually was just 43 only and the bodyweight of the bird at maturity during marketing was only 880 grams. This poor productivity of livestock and poultry was due to

1. Nonadoption of scientific feed management practices
2. Lack of availability of green fodder round the year
3. Nonadoption of vaccination and lack of access to veterinary services
4. Lack of awareness about livestock disease prevention and control measures
5. Non-adoption of concentrated feed, mineral mixture and value-added animal feed and fodder materials including animal chocolates, silage and hey making

Wages/ salary	Crop cultivation	Livestock & poultry	Allied farm activities	Non-farm business	Total income	Average Monthly Income
15537	16424	8434	1776	2220	44390	3699

Technological adoption

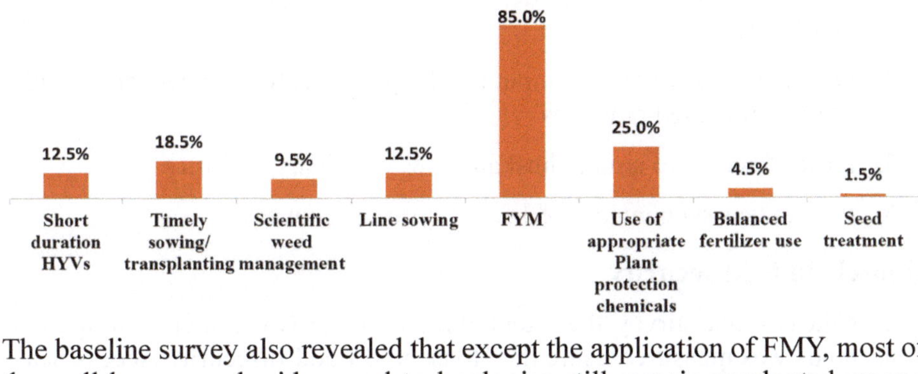

The baseline survey also revealed that except the application of FMY, most of the well known and widespread technologies still remain unadopted among tribal households. Only one-third of the tribal farmers were using appropriate plant protection chemicals, less than one-fifth of the farmers were timely sowing and transplanting their crops, barely one-tenth of the farmers were practicing scientific weed management practices, line sowing and using high yielding recently released crop varieties. It was also observed that the adoption of practices like seed treatment and the balanced use of fertilizers was meager.

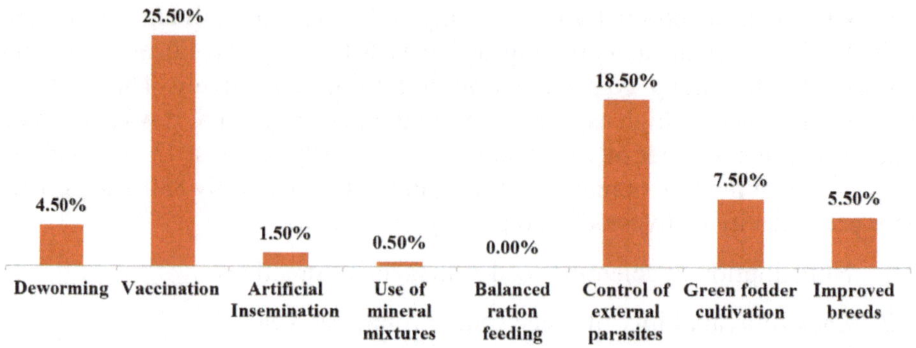

Similarly, in the case of livestock also it was observed that only one-fifth of livestock owners were vaccinating their animals regularly, 18.50 percent of the farmers were taking measures to control external parasites. Adoption of common practices like rearing of improved breeds, regular deworming of animals, artificial insemination, use of mineral mixture and green fodder cultivation was meager. The poor adoption of scientific crop & livestock management practices was due to

1. Lack of awareness about scientific crop & livestock management practices
2. Lack of skill required for the adoption of scientific crop & livestock management practices
3. Lack of technological demonstrations to develop technological credibility
4. Lack of access to quality input resulting in effective /undesirable results of recommended practices
5. Lack of access to animal husbandry & veterinary facilities
6. Poor extension contact and lack of cosmopoliteness

Household food security

During the baseline survey, the extent of food insecurity prevalent among tribal households was measured using the Household Food Insecurity Access Scale (HFIAS) developed under USAID's Food and Nutrition Technical Assistance (FANTA) project. Based on survey, it was found that more than 76 percent of the tribal households were suffering from Household Food Insecurity. Of these households, more than 16 percent were facing severe food insecurity wherein one or more members of the family occasionally had to go to bed without having food for the entire day.

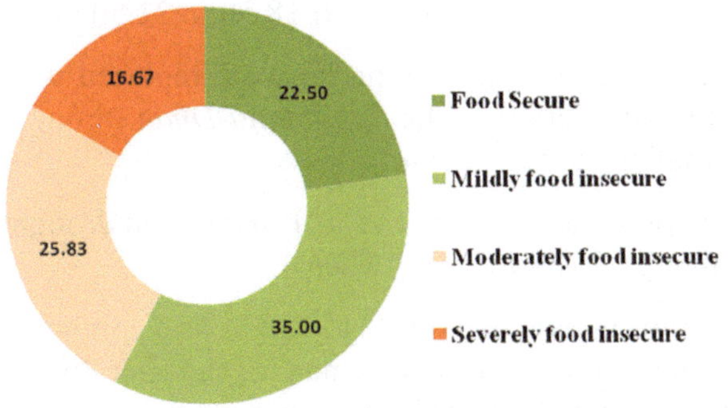

The HFIAS scores were calculated based on households worry for food, food diversity, ability to eat preferred food, meal size and the number of meals consumed by the household members. During the survey it was observed that the household diet of the tribal community was mainly constituted by carbohydrates, fat and fiber. However, the availability and consumption of protein were found to be lower than the recommended levels. Food diversity was also found to be little in the households as a result of which they were unable to eat preferred foods, fruits and vegetables. The lack of protein, fruits and vegetable consumption was due to

1. Financial inability to buy an adequate quantity of meat, egg, fruits and vegetables from external sources
2. Poor productivity of household poultry and livestock resources
3. Lack of in-house production system of fruits and vegetables
4. Lack of awareness about nutritional value and utility of local flora
5. Lack of awareness about the special dietary needs of pregnant & lactating women, children and age-old people.

i. Principal milestones reached in the progress of research/extension work in tribal area

Farm income

The average monthly tribal household income increased by Rs 1512. The total monthly income was enhanced from Rs. 3699 to Rs. 5211. Cumulative annual income increased in target households from Rs. 44390 to Rs. 62536.

Crop production and cropping intensity

Crop productivity in the case of Rice, Wheat, Maize increased by 21.50%; 13.80 % and 32.30 percent, respectively

Seed replacement rate in paddy crop was increased from 18.50 to 32.50 %

Less relevant and obsolete rice varieties like Swarna lal were replaced with early maturing abiotic stress-tolerant varieties like *Sahabhagi Dhan* (drought tolerant) and Swarna Sub – 1 (submergence tolerant)

Rice cropping duration reduced by 20 days (from 145 to 120 days) in drought susceptible Banka district enabling early sowing of wheat

The cropping intensity increased from existing 139 % to 158 % as a combined result of the cultivation of summer moong and replacement of the Rice-Maize cropping system with the Rice-Mustard-Summer Moong cropping system and cultivation of green fodder in waterlogged areas.

Livestock production

Milk productivity increased by 480 liters per inter-calving period, goat meat production/animal increased by 1.63 kg/animal, poultry bird body weight increased by 1.38 kg/animal and the number of eggs laid/bird/yr increased from 43 to 83 witnessing 100 percent increase.

Livestock mortality in goats due to diseases was reduced by 50 percent as a result of vaccination and scientific feed management, especially in pregnant female goats. As a result, the average goat (including kid) population increased from 5.52 to 6.93 per household

The 42 % local non-descritpt poultry breeds were replaced with Vanraja and Grampriya

As a result of scientific backyard poultry management practices and breed replacement, the average number of poultry birds per household increased from 3.3 to 11.40 per household

Household nutrition

Frequency of consumption of protein source like meat & egg increased by 22 %

Availability and consumption of fruit crops and vegetables increased by 18% and 30 %, respectively

22 % of the targeted tribal households have started to consume mushroom as a major vegetable in the winter season

Monthly consumption of eggs/household has increased from 32 to 65, witnessing a 100 percent increase in consumption of eggs

Wasteland development

An additional 85 ha area was bought under cultivation via kitchen gardening in homestead lands, planting of fruit tree crops in wastelands, green fodder cultivation in submerged lands

Community institutions developed

Three (03) community animal health centers were established and 05 sustainable community rice nurseries were developed

Innovations introduced

Innovations like hydroponic fodder cultivation, use of feed block, community rice nursery, use of Taadi were disseminated and adopted successfully

Entrepreneurship development

02 entrepreneurs were developed in beekeeping and backyard poultry 03 enterpreneurs in got farming.

ii. Impact of the work done in the area

1. Enhancement of field crop productivity

To enhance the productivity of field crops (Paddy, Wheat, Maize) following interventions were carried out

a. **Promotion of short duration and Abiotic stress-tolerant (drought and submergence) paddy varieties**. The productivity of field crops is affected by abiotic stress in all the selected districts. Banka region was affected by the uncertainty of monsoon, scanty rainfall and situation of drought. Therefore in Banka drought-tolerant short duration high yielding rice variety - *Sahabhagi dhan* was introduced.

Contrary to Banka district, Kishanganj and Katihar districts face severe flood situations where rice crops often fail due to prolonged submergence. Therefore, in these areas, the submergence tolerant Swarna sub 1 rice variety was introduced.

The respective varieties were demonstrated the fields of farmers in Banka as well as Kishanganj and Katihar district. Further, to promote adoption, the necessary basic inputs including quality seeds fertilizers and plant protection chemicals were also supplied. Alongside replacement of various efforts were also made to introduce and promote the adoption of recommended package of practices including scientific nutrient management as well as plant protection measures. Along with the supply of inputs, numbers of farmer scientist interaction meetings as well as awareness programs were organized to promote scientific rice cultivation in the selected district.

Establishment of Sahabhagi Dhan in draught affected villages of Banka

Sahabhagi Paddy performance in drught affected areas

The comparative performance of paddy cultivation with recommended practices and farmers' existing practices are detailed in the table below.

Performance of Swarna Sub-1 in submerged fields in Kishanganj district

Kisan Chaupal on scientific cultivation of Paddy crop

Comparative performance of farmers' practice and Sahabhagi Dhan

	Crop duration days	Irrigation Requirement	Cost of cultivation (Rs./ha)	Yield (q/ha)	Net profit (Rs/ha)
Farmers' Practice	145-150	5-6	25048	24.2	15048
Sahabhagi Dhan with recommended Package of practices	115-120	2-3	22054	29.5	22054
Impact	Crop duration reduced by 30 days	Water requirement reduced by 50%	Cost of cultivation was reduced by ~ Rs. 3000	5.30 quintal yield increase per ha	Profit increase by ~ Rs. 7000/ ha

Technology dissemination and adoption: Sahabhagi dhan is adopted by more than 195 farmers in an area of 78 ha under TSP project villages.

Comparative performance of farmers' practice and Swarna Sub-1

	Crop duration days	Irrigation Requirement	Cost of cultivation (Rs./ha)	Yield (q/ha)	Net profit (Rs/ha)
Farmers' Practice Lal Swarna	145-150	02	26200	29.9	17155
Swarna Sub-1 Rice with recommended package	150-155	02	28600	34.6	21570
Impact	Crop duration increased by 5 days	Nil	The cost of cultivation increased by ~ Rs. 2400	4.7 quintal yield increase per ha	Profit increase by ~Rs. 4415/ ha

Technology dissemination and adoption: Swarna sub 1 was found to be currently adopted by 56 farmers in an area of 25.54 ha under TSP project villages.

b. Enhancing of seed replacement ratio by ensuring timely supply of quality seed material

One of the reasons for the productivity of cereal crops is the low seed replacement rate. To increase the seed replacement rate, farmers were provided with quality seeds of recently released appropriate varieties of paddy, maize, wheat and green gram.

	Impact on seed replacement ratio				
Crop	Paddy	Wheat	Maize	Moong	Mustard
Before TSP	18.50	18.50	25.50	8.50	8.50
After TSP	32.50	24.25	36.50	21.50	18.50

c. Demonstration of scientific crop management practices

Inefficient use of agrochemicals fertilizers and nonadoption now scientific crop management practices are major reasons behind poor use efficiency and low productivity. In order to ensure efficient use of resources and to increase crop productivity number of scientific crop management practices were demonstrated to the farmers. The major once demonstrated among farmers included efficient use of fertilizers and their balanced application, seed treatment, soil testing and understanding of soil health card etc.

Distribution of Sahabhagi Paddy seeds among tribal households

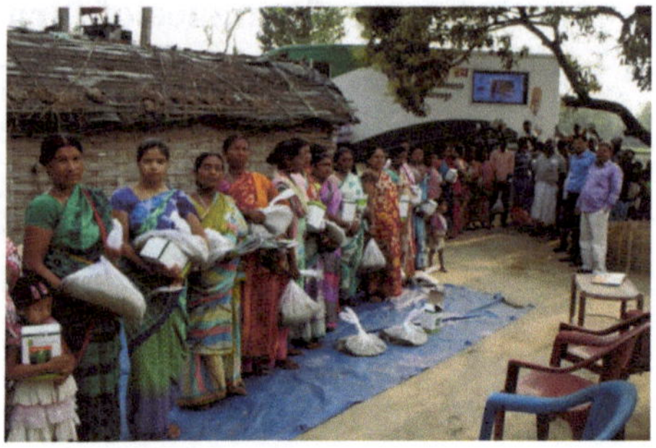

Distribution of Green Gram IPM 2-3 seeds in Panasi Village of Kishanganj

Establishment of Seed Bank

Filled cobs and better yield due to maize seed replacement

Front line demonstration on hybrid maize cultivation

Technology dissemination and adoption: Soil testing was done and soil health cards were distributed health cards were distributed to 175 tribal farmers. More than 35 % of the farmers in the selected villages have started the adoption of appropriate agrochemicals for plant protection.

Demonstration of balanced fertilizer usage

Soil testing and distribution of soil health cards

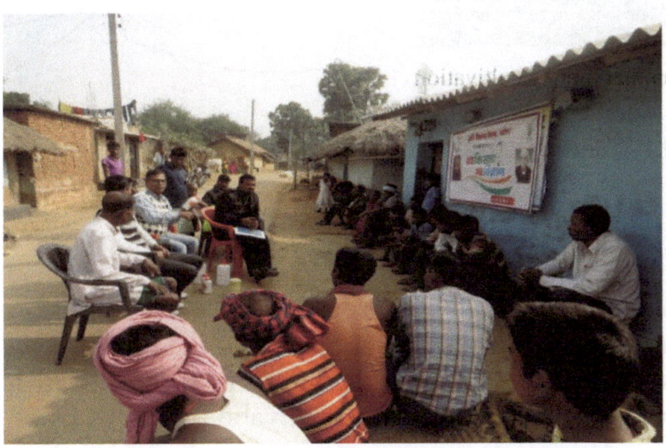

Demonstration on use of plant protection chemicals

Overall impact of the interventions on crop productivity

Crop	Paddy (qt/ha)	Wheat	Kharif Maize	Rabi Maize (q/ha)	Summer Green Gram (q/ha)	Mustard (q/ha)
Before TSP	25.50	16.42	36.25	39.52	No cultivation	8.90
After TSP	30.25	18.68	45.95	49.05	6.25	11.5

Enhancement of Cropping Intensity

a. Promotion of summer moong cultivation

In Banka district where water scarcity is a production constraint, poor cropping productivity is one of the major reasons for low farm productivity. Therefore in order to enhance cropping intensity, the integrated effort was introduced under which long duration rice varieties were replaced with short duration high yielding drought-resistant rice varieties, early sowing of wheat was made possible and cultivation of summer moong was also facilitated by early harvesting of wheat crop.

Frontline demonstration on summer moong cultivation in Kishanganj district

b. Replacement of Paddy-Maize cropping system with Paddy-Mustard-Moong

Similarly, in districts of Kishanganj to Katihar, most of the farmers practiced rice followed by maize cropping system. In these districts, efforts were made to enhance the cropping intensity by replacing the existing rice-maize cropping system with a rice-short duration mustard-green gram cropping system. In this situation, the short duration mustard cultivation ensured early vacating of the field for subsequent cultivation of green gram.

FLD on Sabour Surbhit Paddy variety under Rice-Mustard-Green Gram cropping system

Paddy-Mustard-Moong cropping system

Economic performance of green gram

Cost of cultivation/ha	Yield/ha	Gross return/ha	Net profit (Rs/ha)	BC Ratio
Rs. 12500	6.25 q	Rs. 22750	10250	1.82

Technology dissemination and adoption: Summer cultivation of Green Gram has been adopted by 255 farmers in an area of 95.50 ha under TSP project villages.

Comparative performance of Paddy-Maize and Paddy-Mustard-Moong cropping systems

(Data pertains only to Kishanganj district as the intervention was suitable and implemented in only Kishanganj district)

Crop	Varieties	Sowing Time	Harvesting	Duration of crops (days)	Average Duration (days)	Average Yield (q/ha.)	Net profit
Paddy-Maize							
Paddy	Lal Swarna	June- July	Oct-Nov	145-150	147	29.90	17,155
Maize	Hybrid	Dec.-Jan.	April-May	150-160	155	50.50	25,250
Net profit							42,405
Paddy-Mustard-Moong							
Paddy	Sabour Surbhit	June-July	Oct-Nov	120-130	125	33.8	25,320
Mustard	RGN-48/NC-1	Nov-Dec.	Feb-March	120-132	126	6.0	10,600
Green gram	IPM 2-3, PDM-139	March	May	90-110	100	6.9	11,316
Net profit							47,236

Technology dissemination and adoption: Paddy-Mustard-Green Gram cropping system is adopted by 175 farmers in an area of 55.35 ha under TSP project villages.

Creating Access To Veterinary Services

a. Capacity building of tribal youth into rural paravet service providers

Most of the tribal villages are located in remote areas and it was highly difficult for the livestock owners to access basic veterinary medicines as well as seek diagnostics and treatments for day-to-day health issues of the animals. They had to travel 20-30 km even to buy dewormer and pay hefty amounts for personalized visits. It was also observed that most of the livestock owners were not having any adequate source of information and knowledge that can update them and provide information regarding preventive measures as well as health care practices to be followed.

Therefore to create extraordinary facilities livestock owners at their own villages, the local interested use well developed into service providers by building their capacity to undertake preliminary diagnostic activities and carry out primary healthcare activities like deworming, vaccination and first aid of injured animals etc. Now, the trained paravet service providers are not only providing services to livestock owners of their villages but also earning sizeable income.

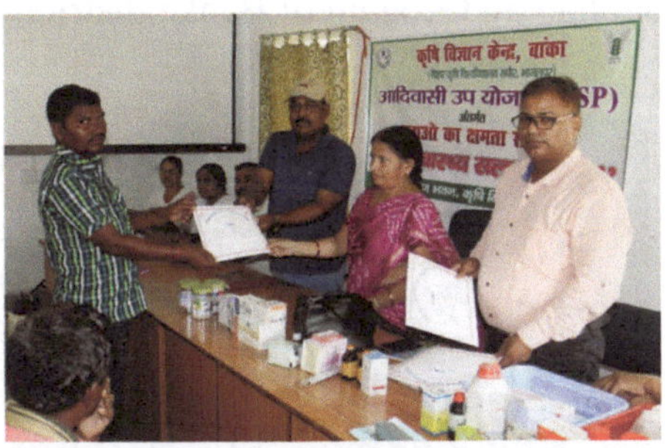

Training of rural youth for paravet skill development

Training of rural youth for paravet skill development

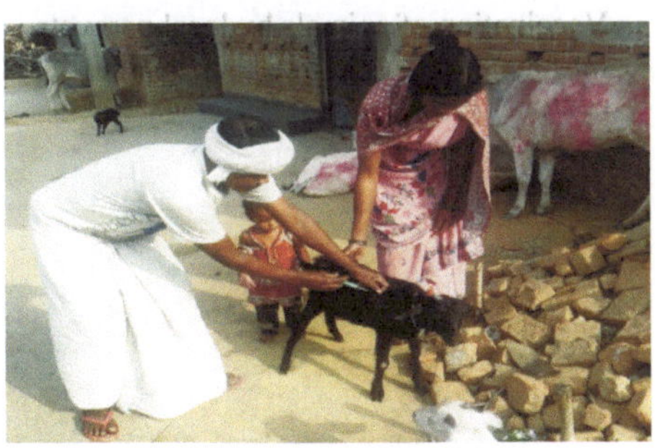

Vaccination of animals carried out by paravet service provider of village

Local Paravet service provider preparing for injecting medicine

b. Establishment of community livestock health centers

It is difficult for farmers to access the veterinary and animal health facilities. Especially, to the dwellers of remotely located villages like Khirkitari who had to travel for 20-30 kilometers even to buy deworming medicine and had to spend exorbitantly on veterinarians' visit. Further, the scientist of Bihar Agricultural University observed that even the animal health camps were less effective as most the livestock were left out for grazing the whole day. On the other hand, locals had no scientific knowledge, skill as well as medicines stock to address the day to day health-related issues of their livestock.

Keeping this in view to establish a self-sustainable model of community based veterinary health centers in a new service model was introduced in which existing infrastructure of government institutions in the village were utilize to establish community-based livestock health centers. These avenues not only provided the local para-vet service providers a platform for delivering services but also acted as a place for storing veterinary instruments and medicine and source of information for livestock owners regarding animal health and nutrition management practices. Such community livestock health centres have been established successfully and already operating sustainably in three villages including Khirkitari, Budhava Baithan and Logain of Banka district.

A view of community livestock health centers

Vaccination of animals by local paravets through community livestock health centers

Impact of community livestock health center on the extent of vaccination, deworming and disease treatment among livestock

Livestock health center	No. of animals treated (including cattle, goat, poultry birds & pig)				
	Deworming	Vaccination	Disease treatment	Other services	Total
Khirkitari	618	425	295	8	1346
Budhava Baithan	298	428	113	12	851
Logain	238	328	75	2	643
Total	1154	1181	483	22	2840

c. Replacement of non-descript poultry birds with Vanraja & Grampriya

One of the reasons behind the poor productivity of poultry birds is the adoption of non-descript poultry bird breeds. These birds not only lay less number of eggs but also their body weight at the marketing time is also less. It was observed that each such bird weighed less than a kilogram and

Distribution of Grampriya & Vanraja chicks

Backyard poultry of Grampriya and Vanraja

Birds can be reared for egg production in small numbers (10 -20) in free-range conditions if plenty of natural feed resources are available. But due to use of insecticides and pesticide no. of insects were decreased also in the hilly area less no. of insects were present. So, backyard poultry in orchard may improve the performance of poultry. The body weight gain was 500g higher in 52 weeks and also first eggs lay was 1 week earlier. The 51 eggs more produce in 72 weeks by poultry rearing in the orchard than the semi-intensive system. It may be due to more insects available in the orchard than plane area.

	Age	Existing non-descript breed	Vanraja	Vanraja in Horti-poultry
Bodyweight (kg)	8th week	0.27	0.836	0.873
	20th week	0.63	1.564	1.773
	40th week	0.82	2.576	3.013
	52nd week	0.91	3.051	3.523
Egg production (no.) up to	32nd week	10	10	29
	40th week	23	30	48
	52nd week	37	50	81
	72nd week	49	88	139

d. Organization of awareness camps and livestock vaccination drives

More than 79 % of mortality in poultry and around 82% mortality in goats was reported due to diseases including PPR, ET and Ranikhet. To reduce the incidence of life-threatening diseases among poultry birds, goats as well as cattle the vaccination camps were organized regularly in the tribal villages.

Timely vaccination of backyard poultry was performed for the prevention of Ranikhet disease at 5th, 21th days, 3rd, 6th, 9th, 12th and 15th month and IBD on 12th, 28th days and 3rd month of age. This has decreased the mortality by 19% which decrease the losses by 1565Rs/ household on an average. The cost of vaccination was 8Rs/bird. So, through low investment, large economical losses were prevented. But the main losses were due to predators (Large cat, Bird and dog), which were major challenges for backyard poultry farming.

Similarly, in case of goats, the vaccination was done for the prevention of PPR and ET diseases. This decreases the mortality of goat by 50% and saved an average 4,667 Rs/family in tribal villages. The cost of vaccination was 10 Rs/ goat.

Animal health camps were organized regularly in the tribal villages. During these camps the health and nutritional issues of cattle, goats, and poultry birds were addressed. Alongside the number of new technologies were introduced among farmers. As a result, the inter-calving periods decreased by 6 months and productivity 322g/day/animals. In the health camp main constraints were grazing of animals from 7 am to 5 pm. So, animals were not available for vaccination and treatment only severely affected animals were available for treatment.

	Vaccination in Poultry		Vaccination in Goat		Health Camp		Animal Chocolate	
	Mortality %	Economic loss due to mortality	Mortality %	Loss due to Mortality (Rs)	ICP (Month)	Productivity (Kg)	Milk Yield (Kg/day)	Days of first estrus
Before TSP	79	6807	82	7282	30	0.191	1.598	223
After TSP	54	4139	32	2614	24	0.512	2.044	137
Diff	-19	-1565	-50	-4667	-6	0.322	-0.447	85

Awareness camp on livestock fertility

Animal Health Camp

Vaccination of goat against PPR in Kishanganj

Vaccination of cattle against FMD

Enhancing land utility

Hydroponic fodder cultivation

The 90 percent of farmers in tribal regions are marginal and small. With their small landholdings, it is becoming a challenge for farmers to manage green fodder especially during summer months in water scare regions like Banka. In districts like banka monsoon is delayed; the number of rains received is scanty and erratic with no large natural water bodies available for irrigating the lands. In such conditions, the green fodder is available only during late rainy season to the end of winter. The green fodder is not available for animal consumption during months of March to July. To create green fodder availability in the lean period of the summer season, the hydroponic green fodder cultivation technology was promoted in the tribal villages of Banka district under TSP programme.

Benefits perceived by livestock owners

- 70-75 kg hydroponic fodder (maize +wheat) from 52.5 sq ft tray area
- It takes 12-14 days for production & saved 95% of water (24-32 lit v.s 276-713 lit /kg green fodder)

- It is less affected by weather and climatic abrasions and It requires less daily labour
- Less wastage of green fodder in feeding

Distribution of hydroponic fodder seeds for homestead cultivation

Harvestable fodder grown using hydroponic technology at farmers house

Planting of tree fruit crops in wastelands and homestead area

A large proportion of areas in Banka, Kishanganj and Katihar are left uncultivated either because the land suffers from extreme Abiotic stress (flood in Kishanganj region; drought in Banka region) during a significant part of the year or the topography of the land makes it impossible to cultivate field crops. Therefore to bring such lands under agricultural use for the production of economically productive produce, a set of interventions were implemented under TSP project in all three districts. With this purpose package of tree fruit crops consisting of Mango, Guava, Litchi & Banana were supplied to the households and they were made aware of scientific practices for planting and management of tree fruit crops.

Distribution of tree fruit crops among tribal households for plantation in homestead barren and cultivable wastelands

Creation of awareness among tribal households for scientific plantation & management of fruit tree crops

Planting of fruit tree crops in cultivable wastelands of community areas

Fruit tree crop	No. of trees planted	Approx. Area covered (ha.)
Mango	1250	3.13
Banana	2520	1.57
Lemon	1580	3.95
Papaya	450	0.12
Gauva	1050	2.65
Drumstick	1000	2.5
Total	7850	13.93

Promotion of green fodder cultivation in submerged cultivable wastelands

Especially in Banka district where monsoon is delayed and later to the harvesting of Paddy, the water remains stagnant in the paddy fields, it is quite impossible to cultivate wheat crop in profitable manner. Therefore most of such lands where the water stagnates for prolonged time, are left uncultivated for rest of seasons in the year resulting in poor land use efficiency and low cropping intensity.

Cultivation of Sudan grass in current fallow lands

Cultivation of oat as fodder crop in submerged lands

Cultivation of maize as green fodder

In these submerged lands, fodder crop cultivation under submerged conditions was introduced. Crops like Maize, Oat, Barseem and sudan grass were introduced under this intervention.

Fodder crops	No. of farmers	Area of adoption (ha)
Oat	12	2.4
Sudan Grass	08	2.0
Berseem	12	1.5
Maize	25	8.1
Total	57	15.0

Technology dissemination and adoption: Cultivation of green fodder crops is adopted by 57 farmers in an area of 15 ha.

		Input cost Rs/ha	Green fodder (q/ha)	Increased MY @ 300g/10kg feed	Milk Cost (Rs)	Net profit (Rs)/ 2.5 ha green fodder
Normal field	Maize	8,690	300	2775	111000	25,775
	Oat	10,110	144			
	Berseem	15,290	372 (2 cutting)			
Submerged condition	Maize	2,705	180	1763	70500	52975
	Oat	4,305	102			

Enhancing of household food security

Keeping this rationale in mind, the interventions like kitchen gardening, backyard poultry, staple crop varietal replacement and mushroom cultivation were introduced in the selected tribal-dominated 33 villages of Banka, Katihar and Kishanganj districts of Bihar.

Kitchen gardening: To ensure year-round availability of vegetables, the seasonal vegetable kits were developed and distributed among the tribal households during three-season *–Rabi, Kharif and Ziad.* The household members were also trained to manage the kitchen garden. To increase the availability of fruits, the package of fruit tree crops was also given to each household which consisted of one plant each of Mango, Banana, Guava and litchi.

Distribution of kitchen gardening kits during awareness program in tribal villages

Glimpses of kitchen garden established by tribal household

Mushroom cultivation: Mushroom is not only a good source of protein but also a source for earning additional income. Considering the local climate as well as the resource availability with the households, the paddy straw mushroom cultivation was promoted in the project area. The household members were provided with training on mushroom cultivation. To ensure initial adoption, they were also provided with basic inputs for the first-time production including mushroom spawn, bags, fungicides etc.

Backyard poultry: To increase the availability of protein sources in the household diet, the poultry production system was promoted. Each household in the project area was provided with twenty-five chicks of the locally adaptable breed – Vanraja and Giriraj. The active members of the household were also trained for the poultry bird management including feed and health.

Promotion of backyard poultry

Backyard poultry awareness programme and distribution of poultry chicks

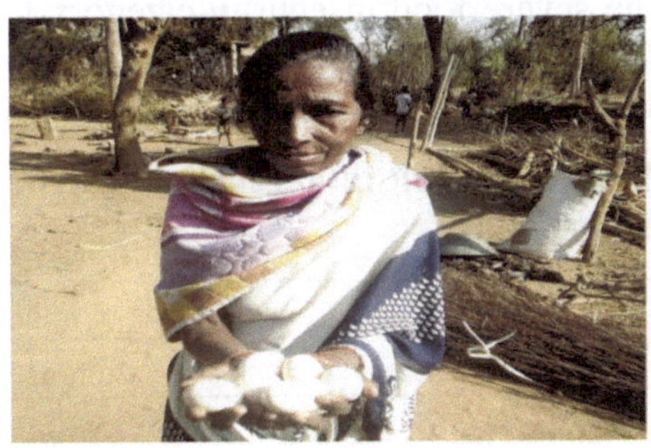

Eggs produced by backyard poultry

Promotion of Kitchen gardening

Staple crop varietal replacement: The project area, especially the district of Banka is characterized by low rainfall which results in poor yields of paddy crops. To address this issue, early maturing Sahbhagi Dhan was introduced that can be harvested only in 105 days, as compared to the traditional varieties that with crop duration ranging between 130-150 days.

Findings of the impact assessment study revealed that, after implementation of TSP interventions, the post-intervention the of households in the food-secure category increased by 9.17 percent (22.50 to 31.67 percent), whereas the number of households with mild food insecurity have reduced from 35.00 to 30.00 percent. Similarly, the percentage of households with severe food insecurity reduced from 16.67 to 12.50 percent. However, no change is observed in the overall number of households facing moderate food insecurity. This does not imply that TSP intervention had no impact on food security of these households. However, the number of households that have moved from the severe food insecurity category to the moderate food insecurity category are the same as the number of households that have moved upwards from the latter category to the upper categories.

Impact of TSP interventions on the extent of food security among tribal households

Food insecurity category as per HFIAS	% of households	
	Before	After
Food Secure	22.50	31.67
Mildly food insecure	35.00	30.00
Moderately food insecure	25.83	25.83
Severely food insecure	16.67	12.50

(Food insecurity level was measured & households were categorized using HFIAS scale recommended by FAO)

Swaccha Bharat Programme

Swachhta Pakhwara and Swachhata Hi Sewa Programme were organised by KVK in project area villages in every year. In this drive, the KVK scientists have organized number of extension activities including awareness programmes, demonstrations and distribution of hygiene related inputs. The awareness was created on cleanliness, healthiness and sanitation in surrounding house and public place of village. The children were made aware about importance of regular bathing, washing of hand, clipping of nails, drinking of clean water, hair cutting etc. The tribal mothers were made aware about the hygienic feeding of balanced diet for good health and maintaining cleanliness around their home and school area regularly. During Swachha Bharat Mission large majority of the households and school children participated in cleanliness drives works in adopted village of Banka, Kishanganj and Katihar.

Innovations introduced

With the decreasing size of landholding and reduction in area under cereal crops, the green fodder availability for animals is decreasing day by day. It is a challenging task to ensure the availability of green fodder round the year especially in areas having no large sources for irrigating the lands. This problem is more prominent in districts like Banka where rainfall is received only during a short period of the year and there are little number of water bodies to support green fodder production. More than 90 percent of farmers here are having small and marginal land-holdings and have no land available for the cultivation of fodder crops. It was observed that green fodder was available only during the late monsoon period and till the end of winter (August to February). The green fodder was not available for feeding animals during rest half of the year.

Therefore, to enable farmers to cultivate green fodder during the off season using the available small space around the homestead using little of water, the hydroponic green fodder production technology was introduced in the Banka district among 12 tribal households.

Under this technology, healthy seeds of maize wheat or any other cereal crops capable of fast growth are soaked in tap water for 24 hours and then washed with fresh water for 2 to 3 times. Later on the trays and jute bags that are meant for acting as base for hydroponic green fodder cultivation are disinfected by using 10% formalin solution.

Once the disinfection process is completed the soaked wheat and maize seeds are spread on the trays @ 0.350 and 250 kg per square feet. After spreading the seeds properly, the trays are covered with a gunny bag for 24 to 36 hours. The wheat seeds germinate in 24 to 36 hours while maize seeds will take around 36 hours to 120 hours. Once the seeds germinate, a water + neem leaf solution consisting of neem leaf juice and water in the ratio 1:10 is prepared. The solution is sprayed on the germinated seedlings on 2nd, 5th and 8th day after germination. The dense root mat develops by 7th or 8th day and the green fodder is ready for harvest by 15th day after germination. Further low cost multi-tier bamboo rack was introduced for enhancing the vertical space utilisation by cultivating 3 to 5 tires of green fodder.

A feeding trial of hydroponic grass on dairy animals for 60 days has shown wonderful results. Two different treatments having the different composition of urea treated paddy straw hydroponic fodder etc. were prepared and fed to each was fed to two different set of ten crossbred cows in the early to the mid-lactation stage. ***Results of the study shown that milk production has increased by 5% and cost per kg milk production has reduced from rupees 13.30 to rupees 12.71. A net profit of rupees 21 /animal /day with additional 3 rupees of grinding cost was recorded.***

Other benefits realised

- Green fodder can be prepared in a short duration of 15 days
- It saves 80 % of water requirement for fodder crop cultivation
- It requires less space-For 1000 kg green fodder: 500 sq ft is enough
- It is less affected by climatic change
- It requires less daily labour
- It offers organic green fodder
- It results in less wastage of green fodder in feeding

Development of successful community-based animal health extension model

On the basis of innovative interventions made in the project an innovative model **Community animal health center for enhancing the access to live-**

stock health services was developed, which can be considered as one of the important outcomes of the Tribal Sub Plan Project.

Rationale

In last few years, the Indian agricultural policy has witnessed a drastic change. The farm policy's goal has shifted from enhancement of crop productivity and production to increasing of economic productivity and income of farming households. On the lines of this policy, the government of India has also initiated the drive for doubling farmers' income. However, with mere increase in crop production, the task of doubling farmers' income seems to be a task almost impossible to attain in the years to come. In this context, income source diversification, especially the livestock sector, has larger role to play. Adding to this, the demand for livestock products is increasing consistently due to industrialization, population growth, urbanization and rising income. These push factors are creating huge opportunities for farmers, especially the livestock owners to boost their income with increased supply of livestock produce to the market.

Despite these favourable conditions, the livestock sector as a whole has failed to capitalise these opportunities to a great extent. Various studies have attributed poor livestock productivity to inadequacies in animal health services. Economic losses caused by lack of animal health services are huge. For instance, In India, inadequate preventive and curative animal health services in case of FMD, Peste-des-Petits Ruminants and *Hemorrhagic Septicemia* together are causing losses worth $ 2.95 Billion. The economic consequence of inadequate animal health services on overall animal productivity is estimated to run into tens of billions dollars.

Currently the animal health services are offered in India by government veterinary officer, private veterinary doctors and practitioner, NGOs and para-veterinarians. However, success of each of these service providers is limited by various factors. Previous studies have shown that success of government veterinary service institutions is constrained by limited funds, inadequate human resource and inadequate infrastructure; increasing preference of government veterinarians to operate in private capacity; inefficient delivery of services and supplies and the relatively low accessibility of animal health services to socioeconomically poor class of livestock owners.

On the other hand, the dominant government veterinary services which are heavily subsidized are suppressing the competitiveness and profitability of private service providers. Adding to this, lack of willingness of small and poor livestock owners to pay for the demand driven services has also resulted in limited reach of private animal health services, especially among poor class of the society. Number of studies have reported that private practitioners are mainly concentrating in urban and peri-urban areas where lucrative opportunities exists, ignoring the most needy poor rural livestock owners.

The livestock health service delivery in India is facing acute shortage of veterinarians and funds. It is estimated that the available human resource to meet the animal health service requirements during the year 2020 will be around 28.5 % lesser than actual requirements. For instance, in case of Bihar, as of March, 2019, there were only 39 veterinary hospitals, 1098 veterinary dispensaries and 1595 veterinary aid centres to serve the health care needs of 32.94 million livestock population of the state.

To meet this shortage of professional veterinarians, various countries including India have introduced alternate approaches for rendering the animal health services through paraprofessionals who are known by different names such as paravets, community based animal health workers, pashu sakhi etc. However, studies have revealed that current realm of paravet functioning is unsustainable as (i) the assumption of sustaining paravet services solely through client payments is completely unrealistic (ii) paravet service providers face difficulties in earning enough to support livelihood (iii) No institutional aid is provided to them for overcoming difficult professional situations (iv) poor monitoring system resulting in resulting in practicing of procedures for which paravets are not trained.

Conceptualization of Community Animal Health Centre Approach

This situation calls for developing an alternate model for delivery of animal health service which not only complements the services of government agencies but also utilize the existing rural infrastructure and local human resource to deliver the animal health services at the farmers' doorstep at minimal cost with robust monitoring for quality assurance so as to overcome the issues associated with existing paravet services. Keeping this need in mind the novel model of "Community Animal Health Centre" (CACH) was introduced in the tribal dominated villages of the Banka district in Bihar.

The model relies on following four basic principles for ensuring sustainable delivery of quality animal health services

1. Developing capacity of local human resource and engaging local institutions
2. Cost sharing for minimization of public investment
3. Handholding support for service providers to develop entrepreneurship
4. Continuous monitoring and documentation for quality assurance

The existing challenges in sustaining paravet services and the measures developed to address these challenges are detailed below.

Existing challenges in sustaining paravet services	Measures developed under Community Animal Health Centre Model
Sustaining and maintaining paravet services solely through client payments is difficult as they are unwilling to bear the entire cost of services and supplies	**Cost sharing:** Transferring the cost of veterinary supplies on public agency funds and that of services on clients
Paravet service providers face difficulties in earning enough to support livelihood	100 % of service charges are retained with paravet service provider to enhance his/her income
No institutional aid is provided to them for overcoming difficult professional situations poor monitoring system resulting in resulting in practicing of procedures for which paravets are not trained	**Partnering**: Community institutions like Panchayats develop understanding with paravet allowing him to utilize existing institutional community infrastructure (building, water supplies and land etc.) for establishing community animal health centre. Handholding support: On the other hand KVKs ensure supply of basic veterinary supplies (travis, vaccination kits, AI kits, deworming drugs etc.) as a handholding support **Documentation:** The paravet activities performed are well documented ensuring proper practice, efficient and proper use of veterinary supplies etc. **Reporting**: Mechanisms were developed where paravet service provider can refer the client directly to the authorised veterinarian in all cases in which he/she is not authorised to operate.

The diagrammatic representation of Community Animal Health Centre Model as well as the role of different stakeholders in operationalization of the model are given in figure and table, respectively.

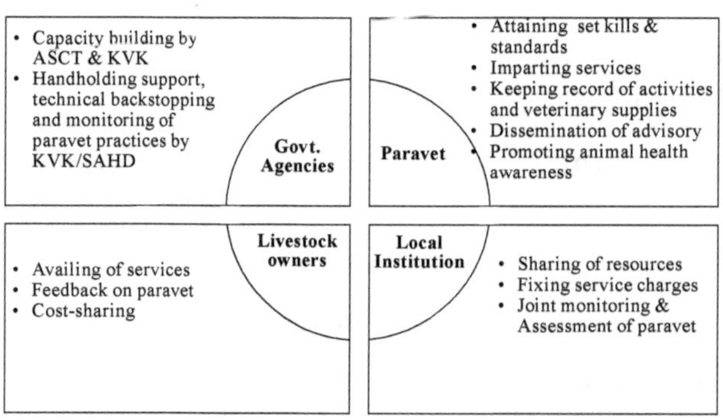

Stakeholders and their roles

S. No.	Stakeholder	Roles
1.	Government agencies (SAUs/KVKs/ State Dept. of Animal Husbandry / of Animal Husbandry / Agril. Skill Council of India etc.)	• Capacity building of local youth with skill deve opment and certifying them for undertaking basic ve erinary practices including vaccination, deworming, first aid of injured animals, treatment of common di eases and symptoms Providing handholding support by ensuring initial establishment of CAHC and providing supplies like travis, vaccines, drugs for deworming and ailment of common health issues among animals • Creating provision for quality veterinary input supplies on a timely basis to ensure availability of service and supplies at the farmers door step • Ensuring proper documentation of activity log of the paravet service provider for
2.	Local institutions (Village Panchayats/ Co- op agencies/Farmers Clubs/FFPs/FPO s etc.)	Allow the paravet service provider to use the existing in frastructure of institution including land, building, water supply, electricity etc. for establishing and operating the CAHC • Undertaking periodic joint review of quality of services provided by paravet • Holding periodic meetings with livestock owners and paravet service providers for fixing and reviewing service charges • Potential local youth (Paravet service provider Acquiring the veterinary skill sets & standards Through prescribed training programmes of KVKs and ASCI • Imparting basic animal health care services including vaccination, deworming, treatment of health uses like dysentery, common fever, issues with calving, recommending dosage of feed supplements & concentrates etc. • Acting as medium for exchange of emergency information between veterinarians and livestock owners Facilitation of veterinarian-livestock owner interface meetings • Dissemination of advisories and creation of animal health awareness among livestock owners
3.	Livestock owners (clients)	Availing of services provided by the paravet • Sharing of costs associated with paravet services (usually the service cost ranging between Rs. 10 to 100 is being paid by livestock owner depending on type of service extended by paravet) • Proving feedback to village institutions and govt. agency veterinarians about the quality of service extended by paravet

Operationalization pilot testing and impact assessment of model

The model was implemented in three scheduled tribe (ST) dominated villages –Khirkitari, Budhava Baithan and Logain –of Banka district in Bihar under the Tribal Sub Plan Scheme. From each of the selected villages, three youth were trained by KVK Banka for developing skills to impart paravet services including vaccination, deworming, artificial insemination, diagnosis of common diseases and providing advisories regarding pre and post natal care of ruminants. The infrastructure of village panchayat in these villages was utilized to establish Community Animal Health Centres wherein the basic veterinary facilities were established & products including travis, veterinary medicines, feed supplements etc. were stored. Initially, number of vaccination drives, animal health camps and awareness programmes were organized to make livestock owners realise the importance of animal health care and to create congenial environment for sustainable functioning and utilization of the CAHC. Later on with mutual agreement, the livestock owners and paravet service provider of the village agreed up on to pay service charges to the trained paravet ranging between rupees 10 to 100 on the basis of type of service provided. However, initially, all the veterinary medicines and vaccinations were provided freely to the needy ones. The paravets were provided with appropriate registers to maintain the record of details of animal, diagnostics and treatment provided along with veterinary supplies utilized.

Impact of the CAHC on livestock health and productivity

The present study employed *ex-post-facto* research design to assess the impact of CAHC programme. The study was conducted during 2016 to 2019 in the Khirkitari, Budhava Baithan and Logain villages of Banka district where the CAHC intervention was implemented. Data related to impact assessment indicators was collected before and after implementation of CAHC intervention from randomly selected 120 livestock owners in the project area. The sample was selected using simple random sampling method from the population frame consisting list of livestock owners who showed interest in seeking the services of CAHC services in the aforementioned villages. The data was collected in two rounds (before and after CAHC intervention) from same set of respondents. The data was summarized in terms of frequency, arithmetic mean and standard deviation. The dependent sample t-test was used to test the significance of change in the impact indicators that has occurred after implementation of CAHC intervention. The details of impact parameters and the corresponding indicators are presented in below.

Parameter	Impact indicators
Accessibility	• Average distance covered to seek service
Affordability	• Ease in seeking animal health care services at doorsteps • Average cost paid per visit of veterinarian • Average transportation charges • Average cost of seeking advisory
Quality of services	• No. of free animal health services received in last one year • Effectiveness of services (on 1 to 10 scale)
Animal health	• Timeliness of services • Livestock population • Mortality of small ruminants

Results

Impact of community livestock health centre on extent of vaccination, deworming and disease treatment among livestock

Village -wise major animal health services provided under CAHC intervention

	Animals treated (including cattle, goat, poultry birds & pig)				
CAHC Location	Deworming	Vaccination	Disease treatment	Other services	Total
Khirkitari	618 (45.91)	425 (31.58)	295 (21.92)	8 (0.59)	1346 (100.00)
Budhava Baithan	298 (35.02)	428 (50.29)	113 (13.28)	12 (1.41)	851 (100.00)
Logain	238 (37.01)	328 (51.01)	75 (11.66)	2 (0.31)	643 (100.00)
Average	385 (40.63)	394 (41.58)	161 (7.01)	7 (0.77)	947 (100.00)
Total	1154 (40.63)	1181 (41.58)	483 (17.01)	22 (0.77)	2840

Village wise major animal health services provided under CAHC intervention Are presented in below the major services provided under CAHC intervention were deworming, vaccination, treatment of minor diseases. Rest of the treatment's animal Services provided are categorized under "other services" category. The most frequently availed service was vaccination of animal (f=1181, 41.58%) followed by deworming of animals (f=1154, 40.63%) and treatment of diseases (f=483, 17.01%). Only 22 times livestock owners sought for other services including advisories related to animal feed and fodder related issues. Across three CHACs, average 358 livestock owners availed deworming services, whereas average of 394 and 161 livestock owner availed vaccination and disease treatment services, respectively.

Impact of community livestock health centre on animal health and productivity

Impact of CAHC intervention on animal health and productivity

Before TSP	79	6807	82	7282	30	0.191	1.598	223
After TSP	54	4139	32	2614	24	0.512	2.044	137
Change	-19	-1565	-50	-4667	-6	0.322	-0.447	85
Test statistics								

Note: All economic losses are in Rs. per household/yr.

Impact of CAHC intervention on the animal health service parameters

Parameter	Impact indicators	Before CAHC	After CAHC	Test statistic value (p value)
Accessibility	Average distance covered to seek service	22.83	6.40	15.21 (<0.01)
	Ease in seeking animal health care services at doorsteps	4.64	6.68	-20.86 (<0.01)
Affordability	Average cost paid per visit of veterinary service provider	320	64.92	21.29 (<0.01)
	Average transportation charges for seeking animal health services	44.17	24.33	7.75 (<0.01)
	Average number of free animal health services received in last one year	0.56	2.63	19.20 (<0.01)
Quality of services	Effectiveness of services (on 1 to 10 scale)	7.01	6.92	0.45 (0.650)
	Timeliness of services	4.83	7.38	10.90 (<0.01)

The average distance covered by livestock owners to seek animal health services before establishment of community animal health centre was 22.83 kilometers. after establishment of community animal Health Center this distance is reduced two 6.40 kilometers. further it was observed that livestock owners have given average rating of 6.68 to the ease of accessing animal health services from CAHC as compared to 4.64 rating do that previously existing animal health services. besides this the average cost bad weather livestock owners for each visit of the veterinary service provider has also drastically reduced from rupees 320 to rupees 64.92 . since the community animal health centers were established in the villages itself, farmers now have to rarely visit the blocker district headquarters for seeking animal health services. as a result of this no cost associated with transportation has reduced from rupees 44.17 to rupees 24.33. further, the average number of free animal health services received in last one year also increased from mere 0.56 to 2.63 services for each livestock owner. This increase may be attributed to ease of access and timeliness of services made available through CAHC. Previously the veterinary service providers were located in distant places as a result of which they were unable to provide services in a timely manner especially in the remotely located villages. after establishment of CAHC, livestock owners can I have access to animal health service providers located in their village itself . this proximity has not only reduced the cost associated with transportation for seeking animal health services, but it has also made there availability of services in a timely manner. Lastly on the front of effectiveness of services, it was observed that the services provided by trained paravet service providers was slightly less than that of services provided by full-fledged veterinary doctors. however, it was observed that this difference was statistically nonsignificant

6

Success Stories

SUCCESS STORY 1

Tribal Sub Plan brings Prosperity to Woman

Savitri Murmu (32) is a resident of the remote village Hulhulli in Thakurganj block of Kishangnaj, Bihar. With the educational qualification of less than matriculation and mere one and half acre of landholding and no skill to pursue a better job, she was striving to meet the day to day requirements of the family. The economic condition of her family was very poor and needed support. To get support for starting the economically productive activity, Savitri also tried with the formation of SHG with group of twenty women from her village. Unfortunately, the group couldn't succeed. Later, she opted to open a small grocery shop and earn little income. However, the grocery shop business was too little to support her needs. With combined income from the grocery shop and cultivation of field crops, she was able to earn less than 50 thousand in the entire year.

But in the year 2017, a team of Bihar Agricultural University Sabour visited Hulhuli village and implemented the Tribal Sub Plan Project. As the part of TSP project, Savitri Devi received training on mushroom cultivation and livestock management from the subject matter specialists of KVK, Kishanganj and was also provided with handholding support in the form of basic inputs required for starting mushroom cultivation. Small successes in mushroom cultivation motivated her to follow the lessons of TSP project. Further, with the technical assistance of experts from KVK, Kishanganj, she stated dairy farming.

Starting with an annual income of less than 50 thousand, now Savitri Devi is earning around 25,000 every month as a result of motivation, capacity building and technical assistance received from Bihar Agricultural University under the Tribal Sub Plan. Besides looking after her household and economic activities, nowadays she is motivating other women in the village to engage in mushroom cultivation and scientific livestock rearing. Now she is the source of motivation for women in the locality.

Before TSP interventions				
Income source	Size of unit	Investment	Return	Net income
Grocery shop	01	40,000	52,200	12,200
Crop production	1.5 acre	24,542	52,450	35,908
Total income		64,542	74,650	48,108
After TSP interventions				
Income source	Size of unit	Investment	Return	Net income
Mushroom	340	15,600	51,000	35,400
Dairy	03	40,500	68,300	27,800
Pineapple cultivation	1.5	1,05000.00	3,40,000.00	2,35,000.00
Total		1,61,100	4,59,300	2,98,200

SUCCESS STORY 2

Bridging the gaps: Community based livestock health centres for delivering veterinary services at farmers' doorsteps

As per 19th Livestock Census, the total livestock population in India is more than 500 million and its contribution to the Indian economy is more than nine thousand crore rupees. Despite its huge contribution, experts opine that, the potential of the livestock sector remains underutilized. The underutilization of livestock resources is more evident in states like Bihar. The state's bovine population constitutes 6.60 percent of the country's total bovine population; however, its contribution to milk production is relatively less (5.30 percent). Experts opine that this situation exists due to lack of awareness about the scientific animal health management practices, poor access to animal health and nutrition facilities. These problems are more evident in remotely located tribal areas.

Banka is one such less developed district of Bihar having a sizeable tribal population where it is difficult for farmers to access the veterinary and animal health facilities. Especially, to the dwellers of remotely located villages like Khirkitari who had to travel for 20-30 kilometers even to buy deworming medicine and had to spend exorbitantly on veterinarians' visit. Further, the scientist of Bihar Agricultural University observed that even the animal health camps were less effective as most the livestock were left out for grazing the whole day. On the other hand, locals had no scientific knowledge, skill as well as medicines stock to address the day to day health-related issues of their livestock.

To address this problem, the scientists of Bihar Agricultural University and its Animal Husbandry Subject Matter Specialist at Krishi Vigyan Kendra, Banka developed a sustainable model for providing veterinary and animal nutrition services to remotely farmers at their doorsteps under Tribal Sub Plan Project. This model consists of three principles, capacity building of locals; creating access to quality input and the continuous monitoring and backstopping. As a part of a capacity-building component, from each village three potential interested youth were selected and trained on the basic practices of animal health, breed and nutrition management including artificial insemination, first aid of injured animals, deworming, vaccination, diarrhea, fever, anorexia etc. Further to create access to quality input for animal health management, the required stock of medicines and equipment were also provided at the village level. The proper utilization of stock was ensured through the maintenance of stock use and distribution records and regular monitoring of the activities through animal husbandry subject matter specialists of KVKs. To run these community-operated animal health centers, the existing buildings and premises of government institutions were utilized.

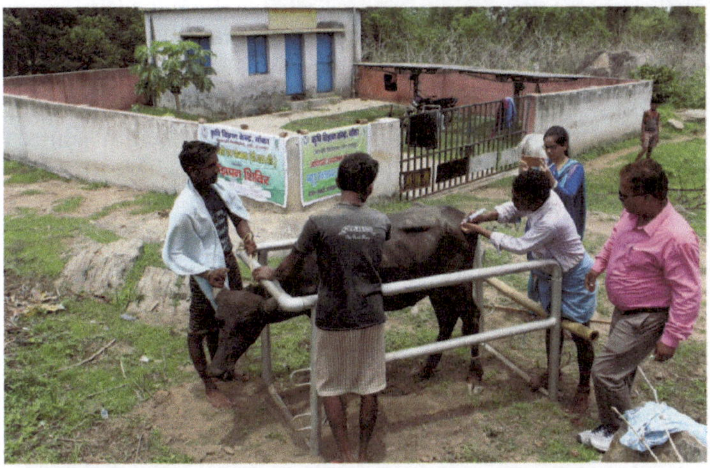

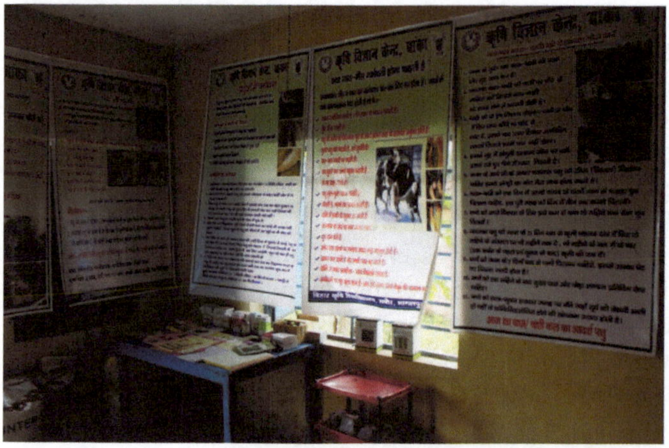

These premises are not only the avenue for seeking animal health services, but the displayed information and banners in these premises are also acting as source of awareness about scientific animal health and nutrition management practices for livestock owners. Such community run animal health centres were established on pilot basis under Tribal Sub Plan Scheme project of BAU, Sabour in the remote, tribal-dominated villages like Khirkitari, Budhava Baithan and Logain of Banka district in Bihar. In these villages, where earlier only a handful of livestock owners adopted the scientific health management practices, now more than 80 percent of goat and cattle owners are vaccinating their livestock and more than 60 percent are deworming the newborn and early age animals. Now, on their own, they can diagnose and treat the minor health concerns in animals including anorexia, diarrhoea, common fever, parasite infestation etc. Without having any need to travel long distances or to pay exorbitant amounts for the visit of veterinarians. In the last eighteen months more than eleven hundred animals were dewormed and vaccinated while around five hundred cows and goats received treatment for curing various diseases. This model has not only delivered the animal husbandry services at farmers' doorsteps but also has developed skills among rural youth and created employment opportunities for local paravet service providers.

To further this model and make it self sustainable, scientists are thinking of transferring cost associated with consumable stocks of community animal health centres to the livestock owners by making them pay partially for the service and product-related costs. In the days to come, Bihar Agricultural University has decided to establish similar community-operated centers in other villages as well under Tribal Sub Plan Project and introduce artificial insemination services also for ensuring breed improvement and enhance livestock productivity.

SUCCESS STORY 3

Beekeeping: Boon for Prosperity

Joseph Hembrum, a 32-year-old *Santhal* tribesman, is the resident of Panasi village in the Pothiya Block of Kishanganj District. Joseph is a sole breadwinner for the family of six members including his mother, wife and three children. He used to cultivate Paddy and Maize in his meagre landholding which is less than a hectare in size. With his efforts concentrated on the production of Paddy and Maize, he was hardly able to generate large marketable surplus and earn enough to meet food, health, education and other requirements of household member.

Fortunately, in the year 2017, the Krishi Vigyan Kendra, Kishanganj started the implementation of Tribal Sub Plan Project in the Pothiya Block. Under the TSP project, Joseph attended the beekeeping training conducted at Sabour by the Bihar Agricultural University. Under this training program, he got acquainted with beekeeping and its management operations. With the handholding support under TSP programme, he started beekeeping initially with five boxes.

After two years of effort, now he has expanded the beekeeping venture. From five boxes now he has expanded his activity to 85 boxes. Honey production has increased in two years from 80 kg to more than 1275 kg. Besides earning profit more than what he used to earn from crop production, he has also created employment opportunities for 03 laborers as well.

No. of bee boxes	Honey production	Net Profit	No. of employment days generated
85	12.75 quintal	82,000	155 days

SUCCESS STORY 4

Income source diversification to change destiny

Babita Marandi is a 43 years old woman tribal from Yogitol village of Patharia block in Kishanganj, Bihar. The main income source for her family is paddy and maize cultivation done in 3.5 acre of land. Paddy and Maize together were no enough to meet the family needs of Babita. Because of the weak economic condition of the house, it had to go through many difficulties. Her family was hardly was able to make saving out of sales from paddy and maize. There were days, they had to worry about meeting health and food expenses of the family. To meet family needs, Babita was rearing only a local female goat in the backyard.

Fortunately, Krishi Vigyan Kendra, Kishanganj conducted a training programme under the umbrella of Tribal Sub Plan in the year 2017-18. The regular visits made by KVK personnel created curiosity in Babita to try kitchen gardening. She was motivated and provided with a seasonal vegetable kit and plant of fruiting trees like mango, banana and drumstick etc. She also received 25 poultry chicks. Since it was freely offered, she also let the KVK personnel to vaccinate her goat against PPR.

With the small successes she realized in backyard poultry and kitchen gardening, she felt motivated to attend training on scientific goat rearing organized by KVK, Kishanganj. After receiving training, she bought 5 goats and 2 cows by taking loan from the bank and started animal husbandry work.

With the adoption of vaccination, deworming and feed management practices in goat which she learnt during the training programme she saw number of goats in her possession increase from 5 to 11 in two and half years. By that time she had already earned Rs 5000 to 8500 by selling of goats. She feels that it is easy to rear goats in comparison to other livestock and nutritional security from the nutritional garden. Now she is happy that she is earning extra income with minimum input cost.

In addition to this, now she has reduced area under maize cultivation and is cultivating pineapple in 1.5 acre of land and earning a handsome amount of more than 2 lakh every year. In addition to this, from Paddy-mustard-Green gram cultivation in one acre of land she is earning around sixteen thousand. Her income is diversified now with goatry and dairy contributing thousands to her income. The kitchen garden has made it possible for her family to consume fresh fruits and vegetables on a regular basis. She is happy that TSP has changed her life.

Enterprise	No. of units	Investment (Rs.)	Return (Rs.)	Net income (Rs./yr)
Kitchen garden	150 Sqm	6500	15900	9400
Dairy	03 cows	49500	76300	26800
Goatry	11 Nos	2500	7500	5000
Pineapple cultivation	1.5 acre	98600	315000	216400
Paddy-mustard-Green gram	1.0 acre	21800	37760	15960
Maize	1.0 acre	25,000	41,400	16400
Total income		203900	493860	289960

Recently, her success was well recognized and she was awarded women farmer award by the Hon'ble Agriculture Minister of Bihar state during a national seminar on Empowerment of Women: Challenges and Strategies.

Appreciation certificate received by Ex. Agricultural Minister, Govt. of Bihar)

SUCCESS STORY 5

PPR Vaccination: A magic wand for doubling goat population

Peste des petits ruminants (PPR) or sheep and goat plague is a highly contagious animal disease affecting small ruminants. It is said that, this highly infectious plague could infect up to 80% of the world's ruminants if not controlled. Goat mortality bought by PPR in Tribal villages of Banka district is a live example of the destructive potentialities of this disease.

The tribal households in each village on average lose as many as 300 goats every year due to PPR devastation. The mortality rate of infected animals ranges between 50 to 100%, with potentially devastating effects on the income from livestock for these poor farmers. This has significantly curtailed the goat productivity and threatening the livelihood.

Therefore to minimize the mortality rate in goats due to Peste des petits ruminants (PPR), a mass goat vaccination drive was organized under TSP project in selected villages. Vaccination of Goat for PPR and ET disease was done at a meager cost of Rs. 10 per goat. Vaccination camps were organized regularly. As a result of PPR Vaccination, the goat mortality has reduced by 50 % and the income losses worth Rs. 4667 per household were prevented. The goat population in the village has increased by 32 % saving nearly 150-170 goat lives every year.